CLASSÉ 1

LES DOSSIERS CLASSÉS DE LA PRESSE ANGLO-SAXONNE

ouvrage collectif

ellipses

ISBN 2-7298-5900-4

Ont participé à cet ouvrage :

Yves Badiou, agrégé d'anglais, appartient actuellement au Centre Inter-pôles d'Enseignement des Langues (CIEL) de l'Université de La Rochelle et enseigne en Faculté de Droit (Maîtrise, Préparation aux concours administratifs d'avocat). Teaching fellow à Bowdoin College, Brunswich, Maine, USA en 1979 et Directeur du Département de Français au Language Training Center, Kingston, Jamaïque en 1982.

Florence Binard est agrégée d'anglais et enseigne à l'IUT d'Evreux, département de génie biologique. Par ailleurs, doctorante à l'Université de Paris VII, Charles V.

Gilbert Bohn, professeur certifié (PRCE), enseignant à la Faculté de Droit de Saint-Maur, Université Paris-Val-de-Marne.

Evelyne Boulet, coordinatrice de l'enseignement des langues à l'Institut des Sciences et Techniques de l'Ingénieur de Lyon. Déléguée adjointe des Relations Internationales ISTIL (Université Claude Bernard Lyon 1).

Monique Curcuru-Villeneuve, professeur d'anglais à l'Université Grenoble III, est spécialisée en civilisation britannique et s'intéresse particulièrement aux problèmes sociaux contemporains au Royaume-Uni, agrégée d'anglais, docteur ès lettres.

Daniel Decotterd, maître de conférences à l'Université d'Angers, publication en civilisation britannique, enseignement des langues et communication.

Elisabeth Delattre est agrégée d'anglais. Auteur d'une thèse de doctorat consacrée au romancier J. G. Farrell, elle enseigne à l'Université d'Artois depuis 1996.

Sylviane Dubois-Lombard est professeur certifié, elle enseigne au lycée privé La Providence d'Amiens et assure des formations au CNAM pour les examens de Cambridge.

Isabelle Genin, maître de conférences à Lille III. Domaine de recherche : stylistique comparée anglais-français. Thèse : « Les trois traductions françaises de *Moby-Dick* de Herman Melville », soutenue en janvier 1998, à Paris III, sous la direction de Paul Bensimon. Après avoir enseigné plusieurs années en classe prépa HEC, au lycée Paul Claudel de Laon (Aisne), elle donne désormais des cours de traduction (ateliers de pratique et de réflexion) à l'Université de Lille III, ainsi qu'un cours de DEUG, 2e année d'expression et compréhension écrites orienté vers la presse anglophone.

Claudie Harvey, maîtrise de LEA. Professeur d'anglais à l'I.U.T. de Dijon, Département de G.E.A.

Jean-Marc Hiernard, Professeur agrégé d'anglais, enseignant depuis 15 ans au lycée Pierre Bayen à Chalons-en-Champagne.

Gérard Hocmard est agrégé de l'Université. Il enseigne l'anglais en Première supérieure au lycée Pothier à Orléans.

Eliane Jaoui-Pylypiw, maître de conférences en anglais de spécialité (anglais appliqué aux sciences économiques), enseigne à l'Université de Paris I, Panthéon-Sorbonne. Thèse, recherche et publications sur le Welfare State britannique (ex : *L'État providence sous le gouvernement conservateur : le cas des personnes âgées*. Revue française de civilisation britannique, 1998.) Recherche pédagogique sur l'anglais de spécialité (ex : *English applied to economics*, ed. Cujas 1993).

Katrina de Mecquenem, B.A. Hons Reading University (G.B.), licence à l'Université de Paris III, maîtrise à l'Université Paris III, DEA à l'Université de Rouen, est certifiée et agrégée d'anglais.

Marie-Pierre Vaurie, agrégée d'anglais – option Littérature –, est professeur d'anglais en classes préparatoires (Lettres (Supérieures, HEC, Maths (Sup et Spé) au lycée Jeanne d'Albret à Saint-Germain-en-Laye. DEA de Littérature anglaise obtenu à l'Université de Paris X – Nanterre.

Introduction

Ces ouvrages de 128 pages chacun, destinés prioritairement aux élèves de classes préparatoires, premiers cycles universitaires, BTS, Sciences Po. et terminales, traitent de tous les domaines importants de la presse anglo-saxonne. Ils comprennent vingt dossiers de 6 pages chacun au sein desquels vous trouverez :

- une présentation générale du thème en langue française ou anglaise,
- des coupures de presse anglo-saxonne,
- un entraînement au thème et à la version au moyen de phrases tirées de la presse et de leur traduction en vis-à-vis,
- le vocabulaire essentiel concernant le dossier,
- des éléments de débat autour du thème abordé.

Ces dossiers ont pour objectif :

- de permettre de rentrer en contact avec la presse anglo-saxonne pour en saisir les enjeux,
- d'apprendre à argumenter et à débattre à partir de notions-clés et d'éléments de réflexion,
- de parvenir à une meilleure maîtrise de la traduction.

Un travail linguistique est ainsi élaboré à partir de nombreux documents authentiques.

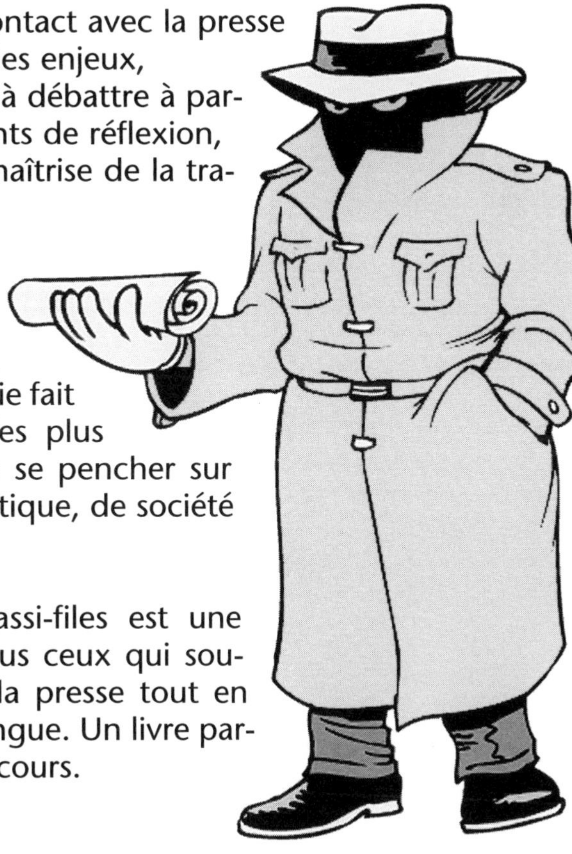

Chacun des volumes de cette série fait appel aux thèmes d'actualité les plus variés et permet tour à tour de se pencher sur des questions culturelles, de politique, de société ou d'économie.

Outil de travail polyvalent, Classi-files est une référence indispensable pour tous ceux qui souhaitent étudier le domaine de la presse tout en perfectionnant leur niveau de langue. Un livre parfait pour réussir examens et concours.

Sommaire

ENTER THE €URO

LE PASSAGE À L'EURO

FACTSHEET

1951: Six countries, France, West Germany, Italy, the Netherlands, Belgium and Luxembourg found the European Coal and Steel Community (ECSC), with Jean Monnet as its president.

1957 (March 25): The Six sign the treaty of Rome establishing the European Economic Community.

1973: Britain, Denmark and Ireland join the EEC.

1979: The European Monetary System is set up in order to help **currency** stability.

1981: Greece joins the community; so do Spain and Portugal in 1986.

1987: The Single European Act **providing for** the creation of a single economic space **comes into force**.

1992: The Treaty on European Union, signed in Maastricht, provides for the introduction of a **single currency** by the end of the decade and outlines some **convergence criteria** to be met in each country wishing to take part.

1995: Austria, Finland and Sweden join the E.U.

1998: A European summit held in Brussels confirms that 11 countries have qualified for the single currency. Britain, Denmark and Sweden have **opted out** and Greece hasn't been able to meet the requirements.

1999 (January 1): The Euro is a currency in its own right; the participating national currencies are no longer **listed** independently on the foreign exchange market; **consumers** will continue to use chiefly their national currencies.

2002: National currencies will be **withdrawn** within 6 months. Final change over should be completed by July 1st; then, only the Euro will be **legal tender.**

The value of the euro as of Jan. 1., 1999

13.76	Austrian schillings
40.34	Belgian francs
2.20	Dutch guilders
5.95	Finnish markka
6.56	French francs
1.96	German marks
0.79	Irish punts
1 936.27	Italian lire
40.34	Luxembourg francs
200.4	Portuguese escudo
166.39	Spanish pesetas

Emu's wings clipped (June 1995)

Governments appreciate better the economic and political obstacles that lie in the path of monetary union. EU finance ministers felt obliged in Luxembourg last week to bury the Commission's hope that the project could be started in 1997, the first target date set in the Maastricht treaty. The ministers said too few countries will meet the Maastricht conditions on budget deficits, government debts, **interest rates,** inflation and **exchange-rate** stability.

The Independent

Fanfare for the euro (May 1998)

The more immediate question is whether the euro will be strong and stable. Many currency traders think it will be softer than the D-mark. The financial markets wag a nervous finger, particularly at Italy and Belgium, and to a lesser extent Spain and Portugal. They have got into the club, say the doubters, only by shameless **fudging** of the Maastricht **qualifying** criteria, especially the treaty's limits of 3% of GDP for budget deficit...

The Economist

The nature of its **launch** on January 4th should not let anyone underestimate the importance of the creation of the euro, the new single currency for 11 European Union members, nor miss its genuinely historic nature. It is the biggest risk the EU has ever taken. It is the first time that countries of anything like this number, size and global economic weight have gathered together to share a currency, and thus to **pool** their monetary sovereignty. It is arguably the most momentous currency innovation since the establishment of the U.S. dollar in 1792.

The Economist

Consumer Paradise

European Economic and Monetary Union will transform shopping. Europe's bloated **retail sector** will be further shaken by the intense competition that's already begun. Dealers are battling to become the biggest, most efficient purveyors of **goods** and services. The few hypermarket and department store chains that survive and **thrive** will be household names across Europe. This brutal consolidation will leave many losers in its wake. But the winners will be **consumers**, who will find lower prices and greater choice.

Time

For 11 countries, a Single Currency (January 1999)

On Friday they were no longer independent currencies but subdivisions of the common currency. Euro **banknotes** and coins will be introduced in the first half of 2002, but already this year the euro will become the main European currency for noncash transactions such as electronic transfers and credit card payments.

International Herald Tribune

EXTRA!!! CLASSI-FILES EXTRA!!!

THÈME

1. Il est clair que l'Allemagne s'érige en gendarme de la monnaie unique, mais il ne s'agit pas de torpiller un projet en faveur duquel les grandes banques et les grandes entreprises allemandes se sont prononcées.
2. Les taux de change entre les devises européennes seront décidés en mai 1998, en même temps que la liste des pays qui seront habilités à participer à l'union monétaire.
3. Ce n'est qu'en 2002 que les pièces et les billets en euros seront disponibles ; tous les chéquiers seront alors établis en euros.
4. En 2002, les Français ne disposeront que de six mois pour s'adapter au grand changement ; le 1er janvier, l'euro entrera en circulation et le 1er juillet le franc n'aura plus cours.
5. La valse des étiquettes sera facilitée par la perte temporaire de repaire des consommateurs ; les professionnels de la distribution disent que la concurrence empêchera les prix de monter.
6. Les banques vont intensifier les efforts de formation de leur personnel ; il faudra procéder à une nouvelle programmation des distributeurs automatiques de billets.

EXTRA!!! CLASSI-FILES EXTRA!!!

VERSION

1. A protracted slowdown would also make it more difficult for Germany to reduce government debt below the 60 per cent of **gross domestic product** ceiling set by the Maastricht treaty.
2. Any delay would have been likely to drive up the D-mark to the detriment of German competitiveness. Many experts, including the **IMF**, believed that putting the euro on hold would have created currency **turmoil**.
3. The 11 euro members' right to inflate, to finance budget deficits by **printing** money, to boost exports temporarily by currency devaluation are handed over to the new **European Central Bank** (ECB) in the most powerful way possible, by treaty.
4. The U.S. dollar, which is overweight in investment portfolios and overvalued, will have a new competitor.
5. It was the prospect of euro membership which split the **Tories** and created the conditions for **Labour** victory. On the other hand, Mr Blair knows that the polls show that a large majority of Britons still oppose joining the euro: this is the one issue on which the Tories are more in tune with the public than Labour.
6. The arrival of the euro is emblematic of Europe's 50-year drive to bury the ghost of two world wars and usher a period of harmony and stability based on common economic interests and developing political and defence ties.
7. The **ECB**'s decision to lower **interest rates** by half a percentage point shows that Wim Duisenberg, president of the ECB, and his colleagues are not bent on deflation nor oblivious to the importance of **growth** and demand.

1. Germany is admittedly setting itself up as the watchdog of the single currency, but there is no question of **scuppering**/scuttling a project backed by big German banks and corporations.
2. The **exchange rates** between the European currencies will be announced in May 1998 together with the list of the countries that are entitled to take part in the monetary union.
3. The euro coins and notes will only be **available** in 2002; all the cheque books will then be established in euros.
4. In 2002, the French will have a period of only six months to adjust to the **switchover**; on January 1st, the euro will come into circulation, and on July 1st the franc will no longer be **legal tender**.
5. It will be easy to bump up prices because consumers will temporarily lose their bearings; the **retail** profession says that **competition** will keep prices down.
6. The banks will step up their staff **training** efforts; the reprogramming of **cash dispensers** will have to be carried out.

1. Pour l'Allemagne, un ralentissement prolongé (de l'activité économique) rendrait plus difficile la réduction de sa dette publique en-dessous des 60% du produit intérieur brut, plafond fixé par le traîté de Maastricht.
2. Il est vraisemblable que tout retard aurait provoqué une hausse du mark et nuit à la compétitivité de l'Allemagne. Beaucoup d'experts, y compris au FMI, estimaient qu'une mise en sommeil de l'euro aurait créé un tumulte monétaire.
3. C'est de la façon la plus forte, par traîté, que les 11 pays membres de l'euro ont remis entre les mains de la nouvelle Banque centrale européenne leur droit d'augmenter la masse monétaire, de financer les déficits budgétaires en faisant fonctionner la planche à billets et de donner un coup de pouce momentané aux exportations par une dévaluation de la monnaie.
4. Le dollar, qui regorge de portefeuilles d'investissement et qui est surévalué, va trouver un nouveau concurrent.
5. C'est la perspective de l'appartenance à l'euro qui a divisé les conservateurs et crée les conditions de la victoire électorale des travaillistes. D'autre part, M. Blair sait que les sondages montrent qu'une grande majorité des Britanniques s'oppose encore à l'adhésion à l'euro : c'est la seule question sur laquelle les conservateurs sont plus en phase avec l'opinion que les travaillistes.
6. L'avènement de l'euro symbolise cinquante années d'efforts en Europe pour enterrer le fantôme des deux guerres mondiales et inaugurer une période d'harmonie et de stabilité fondée sur des intérêts économiques communs et sur le renforcement de liens politiques et de sécurité.
7. La décision de la B.C.E. de baisser ses taux d'intérêts d'un demi-point indique que Wim Duisenberg, son président, et ses collègues ne montrent pas un attachement irrévocable à la déflation et ne négligent pas l'importance de la croissance et de la demande.

VOCABULARY

available	*disponible*
balance the budget (to)	*équilibrer le budget*
banknote	*billet de banque*
cash dispenser	*distributeur automatique de billets*
come into force (to)	*entrer en vigueur*
competition	*concurrence*
convergence criteria	*critères de convergence*
consumer	*consommateur*
currency	*monnaie, devise*
European Central Bank (ECB)	*Banque Centrale Européenne (BCE)*
European Coal and Steel Community (ECSC)	*Communauté Européenne du Charbon et de l'Acier (CECA)*
European Monetary Union (EMU)	*Union Économique et Monétaire (UEM)*
Exchange rate	*Taux de change*
forecast	*prévoir/prévision*
fudge (to)	*truquer*
fulfil the conditions (to)	*remplir les conditions*
goods	*marchandise*
Gross Domestic Product (GDP)	*Produit Intérieur Brut (PIB)*
growth	*croissance*
interest rate	*taux d'intérêt*
International Monetary Fund (IMF)	*Fonds Monétaire International (FMI)*
Labour Party	*parti travailliste*
launch	*lancer/lancement (d'un produit)*
legal tender	*cours légal*
list (to)	*coter*
opt out	*choisir de ne pas participer*
outlook	*perspective*
pool (to)	*mettre en commun*
postpone (to)	*ajourner*
print money (to)	*imprimer des billets*
provide for (to)	*prévoir, pourvoir*
qualify (to)	*remplir les conditions*
regulation	*réglementation*
retail sector	*secteur du commerce de détail*
scupper	*faire capoter*
single currency	*monnaie unique*
stability pact	*"pacte de stabilité" budgétaire qui doit lier les pays membres de l'Union monétaire*
switchover	*changement, passage*
thrive (to)	*prospérer*
Tory Party	*parti conservateur (GB)*
training	*formation*
turmoil	*tumulte, désordre*
unemployment rate	*taux de chômage*
withdraw (to)	*retirer (de la circulation)*

FOR

- Yves-Thibault de Silguy, monetary affairs commissioner: 'The euro could be the embodiment of thousands of years of wisdom and centuries of experience of the economic and social disorder which can be created by the mismanagement of money'. (*The Times* 16/01/96): a single economic regime can counterbalance years of mismanagement by national monetary systems.
- A **single currency** system already unites 11 European states. Others will join: can they remain in the EU and its single market without adopting the euro?
- It may lead to a greater political unity, a more effective union.
- By **fulfilling** the Maastricht criteria, the member states have improved their economic performances: there has been a real convergence towards low inflation, lower interest rates and **balanced** budgets.
- 'Euroland' will be a new force in world affairs: it will attract foreign investment, create more certainty for trans-European business.
- The U.S. dollar will have a new competitor, there will be a counterweight to American power.
- The EMU will stop currency fluctuations, bring savings in transaction costs; exporting will therefore become less costly.
- The euro will, in the long term, bring price transparency for widely-sold products and drive prices down: the winners will then be the **consumers** who will be able to compare all the prices and will more easily find the best deals.
- The European Central Bank, being an independent body, will ensure discipline and encourage faster economic **growth**.

AGAINST

- Public opinions are often reluctant: they seem disillusioned with the whole euro-business.
- The reality of giving up the national **currency** (German mark, franc...) may prove difficult to put up with.
- The basic instruments of economic policy won't be handled any longer by national governments which will lose their ability to determine their policy independently; the nations will surrender a central part of their sovereignty.
- Only the ECB can control the **exchange rates** or the **interest rates**. Wouldn't a political authority, acting as a counterweight, be needed to **balance** the ECB in the administration of the single currency?
- The so-called 'stability pact' has imposed monetary rigour and fiscal discipline; reforms might also be carried out, requiring less rigidity in labour markets, which might increase job insecurity, threaten the workers' 'acquired rights' and wreck the continental European 'social model'. Can flexible **labour markets** be imposed, as western Europe's **unemployment rate** is already high?
- The United States can also be considered as a single-currency area; shouldn't we also acknowledge that it is an open economy, free from **regulation**, with flexible labour markets?
- Winning the confidence of the markets by establishing a strong currency might mean keeping EU interest rates higher, entailing less investment and fewer new jobs in Europe.

THE MILLENNIUM BUG

LE BOGUE DE L'AN 2000

FACTSHEET

At midnight, on January 1st, 2000, many computer systems with two digits will malfunction with unpredictable results, as the year '00' will become invalid or default to 1900. This is what is called the '**Millennium Bug**', or **Y2K** (= Year Two Thousand).

How did we get there? In the sixties, computer science promised to revolutionize our lives, but computer memory was expensive, so many computerized systems used two **digits** rather than four to express the calendar year, in order to save memory space.

However, this is only one aspect of the problem: indeed, the year 2000 is **a leap year**, which was not the case for 1900, so that if a system rolls over to 2000 there may be another **glitch** in perspective. **A leap year** has an extra day – February 29th – and if a system fails to recognize that day, all subsequent dates will be wrong.

The problem is that **the millennium bug** is not confined to **computers** alone, as the same design flaws exist in many microprocessors or **computer 'chips'**, and their programmes. These flaws involve a wide range of equipment from personal computers to automated measurement and process control systems in everything from domestic appliances (such as video recorders) to complex industrial process and manufacturing technology. In short, every **chip** or programme that is date-sensitive could go wrong.

So **the Millennium Bug** appears as the biggest single problem of the computer age, and many experts believe it involves an enormous **threat** to the stability and survival of commercial, industrial, and public-sector organizations. Firms must prepare their systems in order to make them '**Year 2000 compliant**', but this task is not only an internal problem, as the survival of a company depends on their **suppliers** and business partners. International corporations have been working on the problem for some time, investing tens of millions of dollars on computer repairs and upgrades, but smaller businesses are not so well prepared, if only because of the costs involved. In the USA, where remedial efforts are believed to be among the most advanced, **disruptions** are expected to hit as many as 15% of companies and agencies. There is also a gap between the USA or Great Britain, rather well-prepared already, and developing countries, which often lack the means to tackle the issue: a World Bank survey of 139 developing countries found that only 35% have a national plan to make systems **Y2K-compliant**.

Because the potential consequences of **the Millennium Bug** are often misunderstood, people waver between dismissing the issue and panicking - with unpredictable consequences at times, when some Americans (a few eccentrics, but still…), expecting some form of Apocalypse, decide to leave cities to settle in the country so as to be self-sufficient for some months as far as food supplies are concerned. Of course this unexpected effect of **the Y2K** is exploited by some, who are making a fortune by selling wood stoves, or survival kits, or dried food…

In order to deal with this nervousness, American consultants and government officials insist on the importance of informing the public of all that is being done to reduce risks. Still, a recent Gallup poll showed that about 10% of American citizens expected to withdraw most or all their money from banks, and that 17% expected to buy a generator or a wood stove.

Beyond computerized systems, the biggest damage in the USA could well be the **threat** of a wave of lawsuits, as businesses sue **non-Y2K compliant** partners. Indeed, legal specialists predict a wave of litigation that could eventually prove more expensive and time-consuming than the worldwide effort to fix the **glitch**: the cost of hiring programmers and buying new equipment with chips is forecast to be $300 to 600 billion. The price tag for lawyers' fees and compensating people for any **failures** that occur, though no-one knows how many there will be, could reach $1 trillion, according to some estimates.

Racing Millennium Bug, U.S and NATO Worry About Russia

Of all the disaster scenarios surrounding the year 2000 computer problem, few are as chilling as the prospect of a major failure affecting the military, especially nuclear weapons systems. The good news, according to senior officials at the Pentagon and several NATO allies, is that the work is on track to repair and test critical military systems, or put contigency plans in place, before the turn of the millennium. More worrying is the high degree of uncertainty about the vulnerability of Russia and other non-Western military forces to the bug.

The International Herald Tribune

Distracted Asia Ignores The Millennium Bug

Prophets of doom predict that at the stroke of midnight Dec.31, 1999, Asia, epicenter of the global financial crisis, will kick off another worldwide catastrophe.
The first major landfall west of the International Dateline, Asia will lead the world into the next millennium and its first encounter with the potentially devastating year 2000 computer bug. (...)
Some of the confusion over the millennium bug in Asia has been blamed on the region's many calendars, quite a few of which are already well beyond the year 2000. According to Thailand's Buddhist calendar, for example, the current year is 2541.

The International Herald Tribune

A Bug in Human Thinking

Now, a chorus of Year 2000 project managers and other authorities warn that people fearing the worst may end up inflicting more serious damage on themselves, their neighbors and the economy than anything the computers do. Planning experts say those scenarios could include bank runs, hoarding of food and gasoline, fires caused by misuse of wood stoves and generators, and a rise of gun violence stemming from the surge in firearm sales.

The New York Times

THÈME

1. Un grand nombre de logiciels informatiques aura déjà rencontré des problèmes liés à l'an 2000 bien avant le 1er janvier 2000.
2. Contrairement aux Américains, les Français n'ont pris conscience de l'importance de la question du bogue du millénaire que très tard.
3. Nul ne peut dire quels seront les effets précis lorsque l'an 2000 arrivera et que les ordinateurs qui n'ont pas été préparés confondront la date avec 1900.
4. Pour gagner de l'espace, de nombreux programmes informatiques ont été conçus pour exprimer les dates avec deux chiffres: ainsi, "98" pour "1998".
5. Depuis le début des temps modernes, la fin d'un siècle est une période de malaise économique.
6. Une récente étude menée par une société de conseil en logiciels a révélé que les quatre cinquièmes des entreprises avaient initialement sous-estimé le coût de revient pour résoudre le problème.

VERSION

1. While the Year 2000 computer problem is viewed by most people as a software glitch requiring software solutions, some Americans think hardware may be the answer, and are stocking up with guns and emergency generators.

2. In Ohio, a company that makes accounting software is being brought to court by a computer company in Connecticut.
3. A consulting firm that surveyed companies worldwide, found that Y2K ranked number 20 on a list of corporate priorities in 1996, but number 1 in 1997.

4. For several years, doomsayers have been repeating a dark prophecy of computerized chaos to be brought on by the inability of many computers to interpret dates after 1999.

5. Much of the evidence supports the view that the year 2000 problem is, indeed, a big deal, and computers users are slowly coming to this realization.

6. Many companies that had hoped to profit from selling Year 2000 repair services have found business to be slower than they had predicted.

1. A large proportion of software will already have met Year 2000-related problems long before January 1st, 2000.
2. Contrary to the Americans, the French only realized the importance of the millennium bug very late.
3. No-one can say what the precise impact will be when 2000 arrives and computers that have not been programmed mistake the date for 1900.
4. To save space, many computer programmes were written to express dates with two digits; thus '98' for '1998'.
5. Since the beginning of modern times, the end of a century has been a time of economic unease.
6. A recent survey led by a software consulting firm found that 4 out of 5 companies had initially underestimated the cost of fixing the problem.

1. Alors que la plupart des gens considèrent le bogue de l'an 2000 comme un problème de logiciel nécessitant des solutions informatiques, certains Américains estiment que la solution pourrait être matérielle et s'affairent à constituer des réserves en armes et groupes électrogènes de secours.
2. Dans l'Ohio, une société de logiciels de comptabilité se voit poursuivie en justice par une société d'informatique du Connecticut.
3. Un cabinet de conseil qui fit une étude sur les sociétés à travers le monde a montré que le bogue de l'an 2000 se classait en vingtième position sur une liste des priorités de l'entreprise en 1996, mais numéro 1 en 1997.
4. Cela fait plusieurs années que des annonciateurs de catastrophe répètent la sombre prophétie selon laquelle le chaos informatique est inéluctable, à cause de l'incapacité de nombreux ordinateurs d'interpréter les dates après 1999.
5. De nombreux éléments renforcent la thèse selon laquelle le problème de l'an 2000 n'est effectivement pas une mince affaire, ce dont les utilisateurs d'ordinateurs prennent lentement conscience.
6. De nombreuses sociétés qui avaient espérer tirer profit de la vente de leurs services de réparation pour l'an 2000 ont découvert que les affaires marchaient moins bien que prévu.

VOCABULARY

a bug	*un bogue*
the millennium	*le millénaire*
'Y2K'	*"an deux mille" (abréviation de Year 2 thousand)*
a glitch	*une panne/un problème technique*
I.T. (Information Technology)	*l'informatique/technologie de l'information*
EDP (Electronic Data Processing)	*l'informatique*
a computer	*un ordinateur*
computing	*l'informatique*
a computer chip	*une puce informatique*
a P.C.	*"Personal Computer"*
hardware (no plural)	*l'équipement informatique/le matériel*
software (no plural)	*un logiciel*
to log data	*enregistrer des données*
a data base	*une banque de données*
to process	*traiter*
a programming system	*un système de programmation*
overloading	*saturation*
to file	*classer*
a file	*un fichier*
a digit	*un chiffre*
a leap year	*une année bissextile*
Y2K compliant	*"compatible année 2000"*
contigency plan	*plan de secours prévisionnel*
IT integrity	*fiabilité de l'informatique*
IT issues	*problèmes liés à l'informatique*
'Y2K immune'	*protégé contre le bogue de l'an 2000*
a computer failure	*une panne informatique*
a disruption	*une perturbation*
a malfunction	*une défaillance technique*
to cause malfunctions	*provoquer des disfonctionnements*
overrated	*exagéré*
a delay	*un retard*
a threat	*une menace*
a forecast	*une prévision*
to wreak havoc	*faire des ravages*
to damage	*nuire à*
to track a mishap	*rechercher une panne*
to crash	*tomber en panne*
a reliable system	*un système fiable*
efficiency	*efficacité*
suppliers	*fournisseurs*
customers	*clients*
a shopping spree	*une "fièvre d'achats"*
a 'buying binge'	*id.*
a shortage	*une pénurie*
a government agency	*un organisme gouvernemental*
steps	*des mesures*
critical systems	*des systèmes d'une importance vitale*

Time is running out…

Because the millennium-bug problem can seem so trivial, senior managers found it hard to take it seriously, and it was even worse with politicians: only Tony Blair and Bill Clinton have given speeches on the issue. This is changing, and officials in the foreign ministries of the world's richest countries are now analysing how the millennium bug might affect weaponry and nuclear-power stations in the former Soviet countries and the developing world, where it seems almost nothing has been done yet to tackle the Y2K problem.

In the USA, some analysts are quite pessimistic as to the impact of the millennium bug on the economy, and it might represent a survival issue for firms or even markets, as some shareholders start selling their shares of some companies! Some commentators foresee a global recession as severe as that of 1973-74, and lasting for at least a year.

In fact, such predictions thrive on the impossibility of saying with certainty how much is likely to go wrong. Public services, medium-sized companies and developing countries all seem to be running special risks. Yet the greatest worry about the Year 2000 problem may be neither its direct effect on economic growth nor, probably, on its potential impact on human welfare, but on the extra uncertainty it will create just when the world economy is getting increasingly fragile, with crises in Asia and Russia. Eventually, perceptions, rather than reality, may turn out to be the most dangerous aspect of the Millennium Bug.

The Year 2000 checklist:

Efforts to prepare the public for possible disruptions from the Y2K computer problems involve a delicate balance between encouraging prudence and preventing panic. Here are some of the steps recommended by the American Red Cross:

- ✔ Check with makers of computer-controlled electronic equipment to see if the devices may be affected: alarm systems, appliances, garage door openers, electronic locks and other equipment that might be controlled by an embedded computer chip;
- ✔ Stock disaster supplies to last several days to a week: nonperishable foods, stored water, and an ample supply of medications that you regularly use;
- ✔ Have some extra cash or traveller's cheques on hand in case transactions involving credit cards cannot be processed. Withdraw money from your bank in small amounts well before December 31st.
- ✔ In case the power fails, plan to use alternative cooking devices. Have extra blankets, coats, hats and gloves to keep warm.
- ✔ Have plenty of flashlights and extra batteries on hands...
- ✔ Be prepared to relocate to a shelter for warmth and protection during a prolonged power outage...
- ✔ As you would in preparation for a winter storm, keep your car's gas tank above half full.

LE CHÔMAGE DES JEUNES

YOUTH UNEMPLOYMENT

FACTSHEET

Les chiffres du chômage au Royaume-Uni ont fait l'objet de nombreux débats, les méthodes de calcul ayant subi une trentaine "d'ajustements" depuis 1979. En 1998, on comptait 1,4 million de chômeurs recevant l'allocation **jobseekers allowance**, ce qui ne tenait pas compte des chômeurs de moins de 18 ans. Désormais, les données publiées sont celles de l'Organisation Internationale du Travail – 1,7 million de chômeurs, soit 6,1% de la population active –. Si le chômage total n'est pas très élevé, il frappe 12,3% des 16-24 ans, et plus encore les 16-17 ans : 16,6%.

Les précédents gouvernements ont créé l'Agence de Formation (**Training Agency**) au niveau national, et les Conseils de Formation et d'Entreprise au niveau local (**Training and Enterprise Councils -TECs-**). Leurs tâches sont multiples : aider les employeurs à fournir une meilleure formation à leurs apprentis, mettre en place les **Youth Training Schemes** (**YTS**, 1983) et les Employment Training Schemes (ETS, 1988), soutenir la création et le développement des petites entreprises. Dès 1990, les TECs sont chargés d'aider les 14-18 ans à poursuivre une scolarité technique professionnalisée par le biais de la Technical and Vocational Education Initiative. Le budget nécessaire, jusqu'ici géré par le ministère de l'emploi, leur est confié.

Le ETS s'adresse aux chômeurs longue durée. Les stages YTS ne reçoivent pas un très bon accueil : ils sont perçus comme plus utiles au patronat qu'aux jeunes, risquent de faire baisser les salaires et d'inciter les employeurs à prendre des stagiaires plutôt que d'embaucher, les rémunérations sont modestes.

Tout jeune chômeur refusant un stage ou le quittant sans raisons valables perd ses droits aux prestations.

Les Travaillistes, dès leur arrivée au pouvoir, souhaitent que les citoyens passent de l'assistance au travail (**Welfare-to-work**). 250.000 jeunes de moins de 25 ans, sans emploi ou sans qualifications, au chômage depuis plus de 6 mois, ont le choix entre : • un emploi dans le secteur privé : pendant 6 mois les **charges sociales** de l'employeur sont alors réduites de 60 £ par semaine, • un emploi dans le **secteur à but non-lucratif** pour un salaire mensuel équivalent au montant de l'allocation chômage, plus un supplément fixe pendant 6 mois, • un emploi dans le domaine de l'environnement au sein du **Citizens' Service Program**, • une **formation** à plein temps dispensée par un organisme agréé, pour les jeunes non qualifiés.

Un jeune chômeur qui n'accepte aucune de ces solutions voit ses allocations suspendues.

Le programme **Target 2000**, extention des **National Vocational Qualifications** (**NVQs**), s'adresse aux moins de 18 ans : tous les jeunes de 16 à 18 ans, qu'ils aient ou non un emploi, peuvent suivre une formation à temps plein ou partiel pour leur permettre d'acquérir ou d'améliorer leurs compétences professionnelles.

Ces mesures récentes, lancées par le **New Deal** en avril 1998, semblent jusqu'ici rencontrer un accueil et un succès mitigés.

Welfare to work

It will be, says Gordon Brown, a Budget to make work pay. Work is good. When a workless person comes off benefit and is converted into a taxpayer, they gain status and dignity and the public purse gains funds to route into the country's schools and hospitals. **Welfare to work** was the promise which helped win Labour last election…

The chairman of Porter Builders claims he was heading for a life of crime on tough Merseyside streets when his father's boss offered him a bricklaying **apprenticeship**. 'I'm a scally, I'm a brickie. I know what it's like to feel that sense of failure' he says. 'It's a human right to have the opportunity to work. It's bigger than politics'.

The Observer

Whitehall officials privately admit that the results of the first five months have been 'very disappointing'. The New Deal has failed to reach the most disadvantaged groups -the ethnic minorities, the disabled and ex-offenders who have most difficulty in finding work. The assistant general secretary of the National Association of Probation Officers said: 'if the New deal is to work it is essential to engage the ethnic minorities and groups like the homeless and offenders… There is now overwhelming evidence that job placements cut crime among this group'.

The Telegraph

Minimum wage

A National minimum wage does not cost young employees'jobs, says an authoritative report, vindicating the Government's controversial announcement of a lower minimum wage for young workers up to the age of 21.

The annual 'Employment Outlook' from the OECD says: 'the balance of the evidence suggests some adverse effect on youth unemployment… It seems desirable in countries which have a minimum wage to apply a lower rate to young people'. The OECD predicts that unemployment in the UK will start to rise next year as the economy slows, with 100,000 more people likely to join the dole queues.

The Independent

Economic experts are confident that the New Deal will have a positive impact on youth unemployment, hence changing long-term unemployment patterns in this country. Professor R. Layard shrugged off suggestions that the New Deal differs little from previous youth training schemes. He said: 'never in the past have young people had so much personal attention from an individual adviser. Under previous schemes the advisers did not actually have anything to offer. These are proper jobs we are talking about here.

Unemployment is one of the major sources of misery in our society. When people record their sense of well-being, it is found that being unemployed makes a person much more unhappy than being poor'.

The Guardian weekly

THÈME

1. En Europe, des millions de jeunes font des petits boulots peu rémunérés et n'ont jamais eu de travail stable.
2. La législation du travail protège ceux qui ont déjà un emploi tandis que les jeunes qui arrivent sur le marché du travail sont confrontés à des conditions d'emploi précaires.
3. Bien que, dans leur échelle de valeurs, la plupart des jeunes mettent la sécurité d'emploi au premier rang, ils sont de plus en plus nombreux à préférer un travail indépendant à un emploi salarié.
4. Le chômage des jeunes est plus important que le chômage des adultes : on a calculé qu'en Grande Bretagne, si le taux de chômage masculin augmente de 1%, le taux de chômage masculin des moins de 20 ans augmente de 1,7%.
5. Depuis des années les hommes politiques critiquent les programmes de formation professionnelle que leurs rivaux mettent en place : on dit que la plupart des stages de formation proposent d'acquérir des qualifications déjà dépassées. Ils ne servent qu'aux patrons qui utilisent les stagiaires comme une main d'œuvre bon marché, source de déductions fiscales.
6. Le Ministre de l'Éducation et de l'Emploi a annoncé, il y a quelques mois, que les prestations seraient retirées aux jeunes de moins de 25 ans peu enclins au travail qui refuseraient un emploi ou un stage dans le cadre du programme "Nouvelle Donne".
7. Selon le Gouvernement, un salaire spécial pour les jeunes est nécessaire parce qu'ils sont beaucoup plus susceptibles d'être touchés par le chômage : les 19 ans ont deux fois plus de chance d'être au chômage que les plus de 25 ans.

VERSION

1. The **Gateway period** is part of the **New Deal** programme for the 18 to 24-year-olds, a period which includes careers advice and guidance, help with jobsearch **skills**, skills and needs **assessment**, and confidence-building provision.
2. All labour market surveys demonstrate that there is a clear correlation between educational attainment and labour market success: the less qualified youngsters are, the higher the level of youth unemployment.
3. I was told he had been **on the dole** for several months and that he was very likely to remain unemployed this coming year since, as a whole, periods of unemployment in Europe tend to be longer and longer.
4. In France and in the United Kingdom, young people below 25 who do not qualify for **unemployment benefit** do not receive the **minimum welfare support** on the assumption that their families should care for their needs.
5. Don't you think that the distribution of welfare between generations has been increasingly developing in favour of the elderly, while the young generation is the loser?
6. The chancellor's decision to reduce the wage rises that many of the country's lowest paid young workers were desperately hoping for puzzled critics who believe the Treasury's figures do not pass muster.
7. Recent trends indicate a general move away from the concept of age-related pay scales towards shorter-term trial periods and skills or competence-based entry rates.

1. In Europe, millions of young people are employed in **low-paid jobs** and have never held long-term jobs.
2. Protective labour market regulations apply to those already in jobs while young newcomers on the labour market are exposed to precarious job arrangements.
3. Although most young people place job security among their top priorities, an increasing part of them prefers **self-employment** to wage-earning.
4. Youth unemployment is greater than adult unemployment: in Great Britain, it has been calculated that, if the unemployment rate for males increases by 1%, the unemployment rate for young males under 20 increases by 1.7%.
5. For ages, political men have criticized the vocational training programmes which their opponents implement: most training schemes are said to provide already outdated qualifications. They benefit exclusively employers who use **trainees** as a cheap labour force and as a source of **tax exemption**.
6. A few months ago, the Education and Employment Secretary announced that benefits would be withdrawn from **workshy younsters** who refused work or training under the **New Deal**.
7. According to the Government, a special young people's wage rate is a must since they are much more susceptible and vulnerable to unemployment. Nineteen-year-olds are twice as likely to be unemployed as those aged 25 and over.

1. La période d'aide à l'insertion professionnelle fait partie du programme "Nouvelle Donne" pour les 18-24 ans, période pendant laquelle sont dispensés des conseils et des aides en matière de carrière, des méthodes de recherche d'emploi, une évaluation des qualifications et des besoins, et un apprentissage de la confiance en soi.
2. Toutes les enquêtes sur le marché du travail indiquent qu'il y a une étroite corrélation entre le niveau d'éducation et une insertion professionnelle réussie : moins les jeunes sont qualifiés, plus le taux de chômage les concernant est élevé.
3. On m'a dit que depuis plusieurs mois il touchait les allocations chômage et qu'il serait très probablement sans emploi l'an prochain, puisque, dans l'ensemble, les périodes de chômage en Europe sont de plus en plus longues.
4. En France et au Royaume-Uni, les jeunes de moins de 25 ans qui ne peuvent toucher l'allocation chômage ne reçoivent pas le RMI car on suppose que leurs familles devraient répondre à leurs besoins.
5. Ne pensez-vous pas que la répartition de l'aide sociale entre générations se développe en faveur des personnes âgées tandis que la jeune génération est laissée pour compte ?
6. La décision du Chancelier de réduire les augmentations de salaire que beaucoup de jeunes, parmi les moins bien rémunérés du pays, attendaient dépespérément, a surpris les critiques qui réfutent les chiffres avancés par le Ministère des Finances.
7. Actuellement, on a tendance à s'éloigner du concept d'une échelle de salaires basée sur l'âge, et à privilégier des périodes d'essai plus courtes et des taux de salaire de départ basés sur les qualifications ou la compétence.

VOCABULARY

apprenticeship	*apprentissage*
assessment	*évaluation*
benefit cut	*réduction d'allocation*
Citizens' Service Program	*programme d'utilité collective*
clerical job	*emploi de bureau*
Department for Education and Employment	*Ministère de l'Education & de l'Emploi*
Gateway period	*période d'aide à l'insertion professionnelle*
hiring and firing policy	*politique d'embauche et de licenciement*
Jobseekers Allowance (JSA)	*allocation de recherche d'emploi*
Labour Force Survey (LFS)	*Bureau d'enquêtes sur le Marché du Travail*
long-term unemployed	*chômeur(s) longue durée*
low-paid job	*bas salaire, travail peu rémunéré*
minimum welfare support	*Revenu Minimum d'Insertion*
National Vocational Qualifications (NVQs)	*programmes nationaux de formation professionnelle*
New Deal	*Nouvelle Donne (programme d'insertion pour les jeunes)*
non-for-profit firm	*entreprise à but non lucratif*
pathfinder area	*zone témoin (dans laquelle on évalue les résultats d'un programme)*
payroll tax	*charges sociales*
redundancy	*licenciement, mise en chômage (pour raisons économiques)*
redundancy payment	*prime de licenciement*
redundant (worker)	*(travailleur) licencié, mis au chômage*
self employment	*travail indépendant (artisans, professions libérales…)*
semi-skilled worker	*ouvrier spécialisé, OS*
skill	*qualification, habileté, savoir-faire*
skilled worker	*ouvrier qualifié*
Target 2000	*Programme 2000 de formation professionnelle*
tax exemption	*déduction fiscale*
Technical and Vocational Education Initiative	*plan d'éducation technique et professionnelle*
to be on the dole	*être au chômage (avec allocation de chômage)*
to be on welfare	*vivre des aides de l'État, des prestations d'économiquement faible*
trade union	*syndicat*
trainee	*stagiaire*
Training Agency	*Agence Nationale de Formation Professionnelle*
Training and Enterprise Councils (TECs)	*Conseils de Formation et d'Entreprise*
training period, traineeship	*stage de formation professionnelle*
unemployment benefit	*allocation de chômage*
wage freeze	*blocage des salaires*
wage(s) slip	*bulletin/fiche de paye*
Welfare-to-work scheme	*programme d'insertion professionnelle (pour ne plus être "assisté")*
working population	*population active*
workshy younster	*jeune peu enclin au travail*
Youth Training Scheme (YTS)	*programme de formation professionnelle pour les jeunes*

Unemployment in the United Kingdom*

age groups in thousands, rates in %

	all ages	in %	16-24	in %
1989	2075	7.2%	629	10.9%
1993	2936	10.3%	867	17.3%
1995	2454	8.6%	706	15.3%
1997	2034	7.1%	608	13.5%
1998	1766	6.1%	542	12.3%

* ILO figures, in % of all economically active persons, Source: Office for National Statistics, 1999.

Comment on the evolution of unemployment figures for all ages and for the 16-24 age group. Surveys show that the group most likely to be made **redundant** is the group of men aged 16 to 24, i.e about 16 per 1,000 employees. Comment on the economic, social, or political reasons which might explain the difference between adult and youth unemployment rates.

■ In praise of work

Many, in the Labour government, consider that it is 'a human right to have the opportunity to work'. They stress the importance of work and welcome tough plans to deal with '**workshy**' youngsters, who will have to move from **welfare to work**. Yet, many young unskilled people feel discouraged at the prospect of a whole life in low-paid menial jobs. Is there merely a conflict of generations in this matter? Comment.

■ Training & apprenticeships

All over Europe, Governments try to implement various types of training schemes to try to curb youth unemployment. Germany was praised for its 'dual-education system' under which most 16-year-olds work part-time in **apprenticeships** (for below entry wage levels) and attend vocational schools the rest of the time.

Nowadays, too many younsters drop out before the schemes end and many critics find these programs expensive and inadequate.

■ Young people & minimum wages

1) Young people often get very low-paid jobs. The introduction of minimum wages could be a means to prevent excessively low wages, yet *the Economist* asserts that "the minimum wage is likely to benefit current workers at the expense of those looking for work". Comment.

2) Chancellor Gordon Brown declared that minimum wages for 18 to 21 year-olds should be lower than adult minimum wages. His maxim is said to be 'low pay is better than no pay'. Give arguments which could back his stance, then counter-arguments in favour of the view that 'equal work should earn equal pay'.

■ The New Deal

What are the options offered to young unemployed in the New Deal programme? Give your opinion on each of the options.

During the **Gateway period**, which can last for up to four months, advisers help the 18 to 24-year-olds to assess their needs and to find which type of employment would suit them. Do you think younsters are eager to be given advice about their **skills** and jobs? Is the scheme cost-effective, and isn't this Gateway period a waste of time and money?

■ Jobs v/crime

'There is overwhelming evidence that job placements cut crime among ethnic minorities and offenders' writes *the Telegraph*. Do you think unemployment is the only reason for crime and violence among the young generation, and if so, what do you think should be done to find a solution?

THE DRUG MARKET

LE MARCHÉ DE LA DROGUE

FACTSHEET

The drug market generates billions of dollars in profits. The world's consumption of illegal drugs doubles every five years.

The products and their origin: All the products are derived from natural substances, found in three plants, all three grown in poor, isolated regions and constituting a **welcome cash crop** for the local populations: poppies, from which opium, and then heroin is **processed**; coca, from which cocaine is processed; cannabis, which is consumed under various names (*grass, hash, pot, shit…*)

The traditional sectors of production, representing some 15 M ha are:

– The Middle Eas**t** (Afghanistan, Iran, Pakistan, sometimes collectively referred to as 'the Golden Crescent') as well as Lebanon, India and Nepal, which produce an estimated 1,500 tons of opium and 60 tons of heroin.

– South-East Asia (Burma, Laos, Thailand, referred to as 'the Golden Triangle'), with a production of 1,500 tons of opium giving 50 tons of heroin.

– Latin America (Peru, Bolivia, Columbia, Ecuador), which produces some 215,000 tons of coca, giving about 500 tons of cocaine. Mexico produces about 50 tons of opium, giving 5 tons of heroin sold on the U.S. market.

Cannabis comes from most of *the above countries*, together with others such as Morocco, Kenya, Jamaica and… Holland (where it is grown in greenhouses). The first world producer is the U.S.A.

The commercialization: Consumption remains limited in the producing countries. The biggest consumers are Western countries.

The trade is in the hands of very well-structured networks, which organize the transport and commercialization of drugs. **Prominent** among these are the Columbian and Mexican cartels as well as the Albanian mafia.

The **huge** profits generated make the drug industry a modern one, that for instance invests in **genetic engineering** (to create new, better products…). Money is also invested in high-tech surveillance and telecommunication equipments, in speedboats that enable **smugglers** to escape police patrols.

The benefits are **laundered** and pumped into the legal economy of a surprising number of countries. The profits from the selling of crops are also used by local guerrillas and terro-rist movements (in Columbia, Burma, the Middle East…) as a source of finance to buy **weapons**. It is **reckoned** that the Afghan Talibans, for instance, made a profit of $75 billion in 1995.

The means of control: Any control of the market is difficult despite international agreements and conventions because demand is so huge and so general that traffic is **worthwhile** for too many people, because the drug industry employs and feeds so many people that the social and financial costs of its suppression would be enormous and because the profits permit corruption **on a large scale** (for instance, the single most powerful traffic cartel in Mexico is reckoned to spend over $ 500 M a year in **bribes**…).

Even holy wars are expensive. The Taliban fighters say they are trying as hard as ever to **stamp out** opium production. But U.S. **satellite surveys** show that the illicit **harvest** is **soaring** in Taliban-controlled areas, which include 75% of Afghanistan's poppy fields. That helped **boost** the country's April crop to an estimated 3,000 metric tons, up from 2,400 last year. Western specialists who once thought that the Taliban would **put a real dent in** Afghanistan's opium exports – **a supply exceeded** only by Burma's – now see this new group of fundamentalists financing their war just like **competing factions**: with drug money.

Newsweek

Once the **raw** opium leaves the fields, it flows to the West through Afghanistan's porous **borders**. Donkey and camel trains loaded with opium **trudge** into Tajikistan; convoys of **trucks** with false **fuel-tank compartments** drive into Iran or Turkmenistan; motorcycle riders with opium-filled **backpacks cruise** through the Khyber Pass **into** Pakistan. Most of the opium is processed into heroin along the Afghan border or in Pakistan and Turkey. Then it is moved by Nigerian and other smugglers through the former Soviet Union to Europe and the United States.

Newsweek

What a difference a year makes! In April 1994 Dost Mohammad grew two kilos of opium poppies in his **plot** outside Kandahar. As usual, he gave 80% of the **yield** to his **landlord**, 10% to the local mullah, and the rest he sold for the equivalent of $125. In 1995, Mohammad was too frightened to grow poppies: the Taliban were razing opium fields and punishing traffickers as they **swept through** Afghanistan. But this year his field was pink again. How did Mohammad get back into business? Instead of **paying off** the mullah, he says, he is **giving a cut** to the Taliban.

Newsweek

The rural drugs problem is not just a matter of people **puffing on** cannabis **reefers**, though Durham police last year uncovered what they reckoned was Britain's biggest cannabis farm with about 2,500 plants, **handily sited** (for quick distribution) close to the A1 motorway. Harder drugs, such as heroin, are also becoming more **commonplace**. In 1996, police reported that the number of heroin users in Spennymoor jumped from 20 to 70 in six months. The town is neither particularly depressed nor unique; the same and even worse tales of drug use can be found in nearly every small British town and village.

The Economist

EXTRA!!! CLASSI-FILES EXTRA!!!

THÈME

1. Les gens associent plutôt la drogue avec le paysage urbain des cités qu'avec le calme des villages et petites villes de province. C'est pourtant là, d'après les spécialistes britanniques et américains, qu'on enregistre un développement spectaculaire de la consommation et du trafic de drogue.
2. Avec 11,3 kg de résine de cannabis, c'est une saisie record que vient de réaliser la police d'Eure-et-Loir.
3. Cette saisie est estimée à environ 330.000 francs en valeur de grossiste, mais les prix flambent avec les intermédiaires et la barrette de 2 francs de shit est finalement vendue au consommateur dans les 100 francs.
4. Une information judiciaire a été ouverte à l'encontre de quatre jeunes gens écroués mardi à Orléans pour infraction à la législation sur les stupéfiants.
5. La police a trouvé au domicile de l'un d'entre eux 7 kg de résine de cannabis, ainsi que 200.000 francs d'argent liquide provenant du trafic.
6. Il occupait depuis un an un emploi-jeune dans une structure municipale accueillant des adolescents.
7. Fortes de 12.000 hommes remarquablement équipés et entraînés grâce aux revenus du trafic de drogue, les Forces Armées Révolutionnaires de Colombie (F.A.R.C.) sont présentes sur plus de la moitié du territoire.
8. Le trafic de drogue est l'activité de base de la plupart des groupes terroristes du monde, qui financent leurs opérations grâce à cela

EXTRA!!! CLASSI-FILES EXTRA!!!

VERSION

1. Few issues have received more media attention than drug traffic and consumption.
2. In Britain, cannabis **convictions** rose from 18,000 to 70,000 in the last **decade**, but if vigilant patrols were made, the number would fill every prison cell.
3. The police think that the rapid spread of harder drugs is because addicts in small towns have set themselves up as dealers to finance their own addiction.
4. Dealers are getting **smarter** with their **sales ploys**: for example, selling at a loss until users are **hooked** or offering three-for-the-price-of-two deals to **increase** usage.
5. The United Nations Drug Control Program estimates that 240 tons of heroin with a street value of $75 billion landed in the West last year from Afghanistan.
6. Stopping the flow is harder than ever.
7. International agencies have **shied away from** sinking anti-drug money into the chaos of Afghanistan.
8. Dost Mohammad is not going to stop growing opium on his own: he pulls in four times what he would earn **sowing wheat**.

1. People associate drugs with urban estates rather than with quiet villages and provincial towns. But this is where dramatic developments in drug traffic and consumption are being noted, according to British and American specialists.
2. With 11.3 kilos of cannabis resin seized in the Eure-et-Loir, the police have made a record seizure.
3. The seizure amounts to an estimated F. 330,000 in wholesale value, but successive retailers push the prices up and the wrap of shit costing F. 2 winds up being sold about F. 100 to the consumer.
4. The four youths arrested in Orléans on Tuesday have been officially indicted for breaching the drug legislation.
5. The police found 7 kilos of cannabis resin as well as F.200,000 from the traffic in cash at the home of one of them.
6. For a year, he had been working as a junior employee in a municipal service dealing with teenagers.
7. With 12,000 members remarkably equipped and trained owing to the revenues of drug traffic, the Columbian Revolutionary Armed Forces (C.R.A.F.) are present over more than half the territory.
8. Drug traffic is the basic activity of most terrorist groups in the world since it enables them to finance their operations.

1. Peu de questions ont autant attiré l'attention des médias que le trafic et la consommation de drogues.
2. En Grande Bretagne, les condamnations pour usage et trafic de cannabis sont passées ces dix dernières années de 18,000 à 70,000 par an, mais si un contrôle plus vigilant était effectué, les personnes condamnées occuperaient toutes les cellules de prison disponibles.
3. La police estime que l'extension rapide de l'usage de drogues dures tient à ce que les drogués des petites villes sont eux-mêmes devenus revendeurs afin de financer leur consommation.
4. Les techniques de vente des revendeurs deviennent plus astucieuses : elles consistent par exemple à vendre à perte jusqu'à ce que les utilisateurs soient "accros" ou à offrir trois doses pour le prix de deux afin de faire grimper la consommation.
5. Les responsables du Programme de Lutte contre la Drogue des Nations Unies considèrent que ce sont 240 tonnes d'héroïne qui sont arrivées l'an dernier dans le monde occidental en provenance d'Afghanistan, pour une valeur marchande de 75 milliards de dollars.
6. Il est plus difficile que jamais d'endiguer le flot.
7. Les instances internationales ont préféré renoncer à engloutir en pure perte des fonds destinés à la lutte anti-drogue dans le chaos afghan.
8. Dost Mohammad ne renoncera pas de lui-même à cultiver l'opium : il en tire quatre fois ce qu'il gagnerait à semer du blé.

billion .... *milliard*
harvest .... *récolte*
boost (to) .... *propulser*
border .... *frontière*
bribe .... *pot-de-vin*
cash crop .... *culture de rapport*
commonplace .... *courant*
convictions .... *condamnations*
cruise into (to) .... *entrer comme dans un moulin*
customs .... *douane*
cut (to give a ... to) .... *reverser un pourcentage à*
decade .... *décennie*
dent (to put a ... in) .... *écorner*
exceed (to) .... *dépasser*
flow (to) .... *se répandre à flots*
fuel-tank compartment .... *réservoir de carburant*
genetic engineering .... *génie génétique*
handily .... *commodément*
hooked .... *"accro"*
huge .... *vaste, considérable*
increase (to) .... *augmenter*
indict (to) .... *inculper*
landlord .... *propriétaire*
launder money .... *blanchir de l'argent sale*
loss (to sell at a ...) .... *vendre à perte*
pay off (to) .... *acheter (quelqu'un)*
plot (of land) .... *lopin de terre*
poppies .... *pavots*
process (to) .... *transformer*
prominent .... *notoire*
puff on (to) .... *tirer des bouffées de*
raw .... *brut, non rafiné*
reckon (to) .... *estimer, juger*
reefer *(slang)* .... *pétard (arg.)*
sales ploys .... *astuces de vente*
satellite survey .... *relevé par satellite*
scale (on a large ...) .... *à grande échelle*
shy away from (to) .... *renoncer (par crainte) à*
site (to) .... *situer, localiser*
smart (adj) .... *(US) astucieux*
smuggler .... *contrebandier*
soar (to) .... *grimper en flêche*
sow (to) wheat .... *semer du blé*
stamp out (to) .... *éradiquer*
supply .... *l'offre*
sweep though (to) .... *se répandre à travers*
the yield .... *ce que cela rapporte*
trudge (to) .... *crapahuter*
weapons .... *des armes*
worthwhile .... *qui en vaut la peine*

■ All the following suggestions have been made at some time or other - and in some cases have even been tested - so as to try and stop the drugs traffic.

Examine the feasability and practical aspects of each of them and discuss its desirability and chances of success.

1. Prohibition generates traffics. The legalisation of drugs and the liberalisation of the market would cut the traffic.
2. If drugs were legalized and the market liberated, the sales taxes would bring extra revenue to the governments, possibly enabling them to launch innovative social policies.
3. The United Nations should take the initiative of an all-out war against drug traffickers and send troops to destroy illegal crops.
4. The United Nations should launch a programme in order to encourage farmers to grow other crops and to give them financial compensation if they decide to stop growing illegal crops.
5. The United Nations should vote an embargo on the exports of all the countries suspected of producing or exporting drugs.
6. Strict **customs** controls should be set up at the borders and in each port and airport so as to check all potential carriers.
7. The death penalty should be reintroduced for all convicted drug traffickers and dealers.

■ Would *you* have a suggestion to make? Explain it in no more than 60 words.

AMERICA, RIGHT OR WRONG?

L'AMÉRIQUE A-T-ELLE RAISON OU TORT ?

FACTSHEET

Some of the early historians believed Americans were a Chosen People in the Biblical sense and described the birth of the United States of America as a unique historic experience. The term, American 'exceptionalism' was coined because the country created its own civilization pattern in a land of natural riches. Such a combination catches fire in the world's imagination and **spawns** reactions of love or hate.

The myth of America as the 'garden of the world' was stressed by H. D. Thoreau. According to him, the American wilderness was a formidable reservoir for the new democracy. But already aware of its degradation by man, he warned his contemporaries against their short-sightedness.

The **worship** of the Constitution is part of American tradition. It has provided the basis for political stability, individual freedom, economic growth and social progress. The American constitution, ratified and **implemented** on March 4th, 1789, owes its staying power to its simplicity and flexibility. It has been the cement for peoples escaping their past because of poverty, or intolerance. They were proud to **abide by** the Constitution in order to invent a new country and say: 'This is America.'

Americans can boast that their motto '*E Pluribus Unum*' has become a fact. Throughout the 19th century and on into the 20th century, an endless stream of immigrants contributed their skills and their cultural heritages to the growing nation. From a purely **WASP** society, America has become a **'tossed salad'** in which Blacks, Latinos and Asians may constitute a majority of the nation's children in the future. The present cult of ethnicity or 'multiculturalism' crystallizes differences between ethnic groups and intensifies tensions. **Affirmative Action** is now thought to be **Reverse Discrimination**. **Political Correctness**, devised not to offend minorities can be felt as an **encroachment on** the freedom of speech and as mere hypocrisy.

In fact the US is a land of plenty where material prosperity has always been considered as God's blessing to the country and its imaginative **entrepreneurs**. The American Constitution is the only one in the world to mention **'the pursuit of happiness.'** Each man by pursuing his self-interest is thought to help the common good. Liberalism is linked with an emphasis on a limited federal government and on contempt for bureaucrats. But greedy materialism, corrupt wealth and social inequalities **plague** the system.

The American attitude towards foreign nations is closely tied historically to the US geographical position. It used to be very far from any other country. Thus the US was **isolationist** at times. However, because it is convinced that it **embodies** democracy, it often behaves as the **watch-dog** of the world. Its current wish to help nations where human rights are violated is no easy task and American international involvement is often criticized.

The US is a country of paradoxes, offering the best and the worst. It feels it can bring freedom and happiness to the world. Its literature and art endlessly question the American Dream but one cannot remain indifferent to America's extraordinary dynamism.

3

E Pluribus Unum?

It is possible that the first colonist on these shores, as soon as he got the seaweed out of his shoes, turned and shouted toward the old country, 'No more, now-that's enough!' The extraordinary ferocity with which each colony resisted newcomers lasted until finally the immigration laws slowed the river of strangers to a stream and then to a drip. Then we arrived at a curious and ridiculous position: the very men who were most influential to getting the restrictive immigration laws passed were forced **to advocate** the admission of new cheap **labor**, and in some cases to admit it illegally.

John Steinbeck, 'America and Americans', (Bouanza Books, N.Y. 1966)

6

American Pastoral

All that normalcy interrupted by murder. All the small problems any family expects to encounter exaggerated by something so impossible to reconcile. The disruption of the anticipated American future that was simply to have unrolled out of the solid American past, out of each generation's getting smarter, out of each generation's breaking away from the parochialism a little further, out of the desire to go the limit in America with your rights, forming yourself as an ideal person, who frees himself of the pre-America insecurities and the old, constraining obsessions so as to live unapologetically as an equal among equals… And then the daughter who transports you out of the longed for American pastoral and into everything that is its antithesis and its enemy, into the fury, the violence, and the degradation of the counterpastoral-into the indigenous American **berserk**.

Philip Roth, 'American Pastoral', (Vintage Books, N.Y. 1997)

2

Emerson's 'cultural declaration of Independence'

Our day of dependence, our long **apprenticeship** to the learning of other lands, draws to a close. The millions that around us are rushing into life, cannot always be fed on the only remains of foreign **harvests**. Events, actions arise, that must be sung, that will sing themselves.

'The American Scholar' in Ralph Waldo Emerson, Selected Essays (Penguin Books, N.Y. 1982), pp. 83-84

4

The Lost Continent

In high school, I shared a locker with a Dutch exchange student and I remember him asking me one day why everybody, absolutely everybody wanted him to like America better than the Netherlands. 'Holland is my home,' he said. 'Why can't people understand that it's where I want to live?' I considered his point. 'Yes,' I said, 'but deep down, Anton, wouldn't you really rather live here?' And funnily enough in the end, he decided he did. The last I heard he was a successful **realtor** in Florida, driving a Porsche, wearing sunglasses and saying, 'Hey, what's happening?'

Bill Bryson, 'The lost Continent', (Black Swan, London 1995)

1

The Declaration of Independence

We hold these truths to be self-evident, that all men are created equal, that they are **endowed** by their Creator **with** certain unalienable rights, that among these are Life, Liberty, and the pursuit of Happiness.

Preambule

5

White Noise

'I have trouble imagining death at that income level,' she said.
'Maybe there is no death as we know it. Just documents changing hands.'

Don De Lillo, 'White Noise', (Viking Penguin N.Y., 1956)

THÈME

1. Depuis la chute de l'U.R.S.S., il n'y a plus qu'une seule superpuissance dans le monde, ce qui rend la diplomatie américaine d'autant plus compliquée.
2. Les meurtres, les viols, les foyers avec une femme seule sont beaucoup plus nombreux aux U.S.A. que dans l'Union Européenne.
3. Jamais la domination des USA n'a été aussi totale : militaire, technologique, culturelle…
4. Tout comme l'Europe a besoin de l'Amérique pour se persuader que le plein emploi est possible, les États-Unis ont besoin de l'Europe et de sa vision d'une société plus égalitaire.
5. Dans le passé, les Américains ont voulu se faire aimer de l'étranger : lorsqu'ils voyageaient, ils donnaient pourboires, salaires, compliments à outrance. Ils ont mis du temps à comprendre que quiconque veut être aimé à tout prix, attire généralement l'inimitié et le mépris.
6. Les années d'isolationnisme de l'Amérique s'expliquent par la peur de l'inconnu et par le mépris que les Européens portaient au soi-disant manque de raffinement des Américains.

VERSION

Phrases tirées de John Steinbeck, *America and Americans*
(*The Viking Press Inc.*, New York)

1. Americans treasure the knowledge that they live close to nature, but fewer and fewer farmers feed more and more people; and as soon as we can afford to, we eat out of cans and buy frozen TV dinners.
2. We fancy ourselves as hard-headed realists, but we will buy anything we see advertised, particulartly on television. (p. 31)
3. Since a family's image of success in the world, or status, is to some extent dependent on the kind of car the man drives, he was forced to buy a new one whether he needed it or not. (p. 32)
4. The giants of money were usually the sons of poor men who clawed and grappled their way to great fortune, driven by memory of poverty and hardship. (p. 68)
5. I think that the picture of America and the Americans which is **branded** on the minds of foreigners is **derived** in very large part **from** our novels, our short-stories and particularly from our moving pictures. (p. 136)
6. In Europe, a journalist is looked upon as a second or third-rate writer. In America, on the contrary, journalism is not only a respected profession, but is considered the training ground of any good American author. (p.133)

1. Since the downfall of the U.S.S.R., there has been but one superpower, which makes American diplomacy all the trickier.
2. There are far more murders, rapes and **households** maintained by women in the U.S.A. than in the European Community.
3. Never has US supremacy been so complete: it is military, technological as well as cultural.
4. Just as Europe needs America to be convinced that full employment is feasible, the U.S.A. needs Europe for its vision of a more egalitarian society.
5. In the past, Americans wanted foreigners to love them: when they travelled, they overtipped, overpaid and overpraised. It took them some time to realize that whoever desperately wants to be loved, usually draws dislike or contempt.
6. The years of America's isolationism can be accounted for by the fear of the unknown and by the fact that Europeans looked down upon the Americans' so-called lack of refinement.

1. Les Américains chérissent l'idée qu'ils vivent près de la nature, mais un nombre toujours plus petit de paysans nourrit un nombre toujours plus grand de gens ; et dès que nous pouvons nous l'offrir, nous nous nourrissons de boîtes de conserves et achetons des repas surgelés pour nos soirées télévision.
2. Nous nous imaginons être des réalistes qui gardons la tête froide, mais nous achetons tout ce dont on fait la publicité, surtout à la télévision.
3. Puisque pour une famille, la marque du succès, ou du statut social dans le monde dépend dans une certaine mesure du genre de voiture que l'homme conduit, il fut forcé d'en acheter une neuve qu'il en ait eu ou non besoin.
4. Les géants de l'argent étaient généralement les fils de gens pauvres qui s'étaient hissés au haut de l'échelle à la force du poignet, poussés par le souvenir de leur pauvreté et de leurs difficultés.
5. Je pense que l'image de marque de l'Amérique et du peuple américain gravée dans l'esprit des étrangers est tirée en grande partie de nos romans, nouvelles, et surtout de nos films.
6. En Europe, on méprise un journaliste en le prenant pour un écrivain de deuxième ou troisième ordre. En Amérique, par contre, le journalisme n'est pas seulement considéré comme une profession respectable mais aussi comme l'apprentissage de tout bon auteur américain.

VOCABULARY

abide by (to)	*se conformer à, respecter*
advocate (to)	*recommander*
Affirmative Action	*discrimination positive : programme instauré dans les années 1970 pour obliger les universités et administrations à engager des minorités (politique de quotas)*
apprenticeship	*apprentissage*
a berserk	*un fou furieux (familier)*
a brand	*une marque*
to brand (to)	*étiqueter, graver*
contempt	*mépris*
derive from (to)	*provenir de, dériver de*
embody (to)	*incarner*
an encroachment on	*un empiètement sur*
endow with (to)	*douer de*
harvest	*moisson*
household	*foyer*
implement (to)	*appliquer, mettre en œuvre*
income differential	*écart de revenu*
labor	*main-d'œuvre*
life expectancy	*l'espérance de vie*
a mixed salad	*une salade composée : ce terme s'oppose à celui de 'melting pot' (creuset) pour indiquer que les ethnies ne fusionnent plus mais gardent leur identité.*
per capita	*par personne*
plague (to)	*miner, nuire à*
Political Correctness	*le "politiquement correct" : nouveau langage pour ne pas offenser : minorités raciales, femmes, personnes agées... (ex. an African-American : un Noir)*
poverty line	*seuil de pauvreté*
the pursuit of happiness	*la poursuite du bohneur*
a realtor	*agent immobilier*
reverse discrimination	*discrimination à rebours*
social coverage	*couverture sociale*
spawn (to)	*engendrer*
a start-up	*affaire qui démarre*
SWOT	*'Strengths, Weaknesses, Opportunities, Threats', terme économique utilisé par les entreprises qui doivent analyser tous ces paramètres pour ajuster leur politique*
unemployment rate	*taux de chômage*
WASP = White Anglo Saxon Protestant	*ce terme caractérise les premiers colons américains ; il désigne l'aristocratie américaine*
a watch-dog	*chien de garde*
worship	*culte*

AMERICA RIGHT OR WRONG?
(Figures taken in *Capital,* n°93, June 1999)

USA	Europe	
Population (million)	270	376
less than 15 years old	22%	17%
more than 65 years old	13%	15%
having a job	73.5%	60.4%
Unemployment rate	4.5%	
Life expectancy (years)	76.4	79.9
Number of work hours per week	42	39
Cost of an hour of work in industry, social coverage included in French Francs	133.8	142.3
Number of students per 1,000 youngsters from 15 to 29 years old	260	151
Rate of start-ups: from 1994 to 1998	11.4%	9.9%
Average income per capita (in French Francs, in 1998)	157,463	111,627
Number of medical doctors per 1,000 inhabitants	245	291
Percentage of people living under the poverty line	14.5%	13.6%
Income differential between the richest 20% and the poorest 20%	From 1 to 9	From 1 to 7
Number of people in jail per 100,000 inhabitants	630	87
Number of murders per 100,000 inhabitants	12.4	1.7

In order to comment upon this table use the following phrases:

- To express contrast between the US and Europe:

  Prepositions: unlike, contrary to; adverbs: on the contrary, contrariwise, on one hand... on the other hand; conjunctions: whereas, while, whilst; pronouns: the former... the latter.

- To qualify America's strong or weak points: (Try to make a **SWOT** analysis):

  Adverbs: however, nevertheless, nonetheless, and yet, all the same, still, though (at the end of the sentence.)

  Conjunctions: although, though (at the beginning of the sentence) even though, even if

  Let alone; it needs qualifying; up to a point; to a limited extent; in so far as; unless; provided that, granted that.

ORGANIC FOOD

LA NOURRITURE BIOLOGIQUE

FACTSHEET

Mad Cow disease, **C.J.D.**, E coli and genetically modified organisms have **fuelled** the green movement to press on with its quest for unadulterated, unpoisoned, unengineered fruit, vegetables, **dairy produce**, meat and fish. In spite of its somewhat off-putting appearance, **organic** food is the latest craze in British supermarkets.

The basic idea is that what is natural is healthy and better. In essence, organic means that **crops** are grown in a way that excludes the use of artificial pesticides, chemicals, **fertilisers** and genetic modification. The definition forbids growth hormones, non-organic **feed** and the routine use of medicines for animals.

The word organic cannot be used unless products have been produced to full organic standards by a registered grower or farmer. The largest of the six organic certification **schemes** in the U.K. is the **Soil** Association.

According to the **Soil** Association, 0.5% of British farms are registered as organic. Any farmer starting along the organic path must **ensure** that his land has not been treated with artificial fertilisers, pesticides or fungicides for at least two years, although organic associations admit that some chemicals can **linger** in the **soil** for up to two decades. The unprofitable two-year conversion period is **a stumbling block** for a number of farmers who would like to switch to organic farming. The **upshot** is that 70% of the organic produce sold in Britain is imported.

The nature of organic farming – it is usually more labour-intensive and **yields** can sometimes be lower – leads to organic produce being more costly. Some supermarkets accept lower profit margins on organic foods in an effort to show that they are environment-friendly.

Organic Farmers and Growers, a co-operative, claims that people want organic food for a mixture of reasons. 'They want the **flavour**, and they don't want the chemicals – perhaps they suffer from allergies. Others have environmental beliefs or concern for animal welfare.'

The **animal welfare lobby** can indeed find cause for celebration in the living conditions of, for example, organic chickens. Unlike **battery hens**, organic **poultry** is **reared** with plenty of space and light, and on an all-natural organic diet. They have freedom to **roam** and **forage** on grassland during daylight hours and have well-ventilated chicken sheds for shelter at night.

Above all, there is no doubt that there is a real market for organic produce in spite of the fact that it looks a little different to produce grown conventionally. The natural imperfections are made up for by improved **flavour** and texture which are said to be the result of the natural farming methods enriching the **soil** and minimising pollution. Research suggests that 80% of customers would buy organic food if it were readily available, and at the same price as non-organic produce. Sainsbury's already sells more than £1 million-worth a week. This year Tesco's has seen a 100% increase in such products.

Hungry for organic food

Organic food is becoming so popular that demand now far **outstrips** supply, and sales have **soared.** The impetus for growth has come from the current trend towards healthier lifestyles, including **diet** and exercise, the consumer awareness of green issues and the high level of media attention surrounding recent health scares.

The Daily Mail

Supermarkets, serving a huge, undiscriminating market, find organic produce difficult and relatively expensive to sell. Take carrots: from Organic Direct, in Wales, they cost 26p a **lb** (of which the grower gets 18p). Yet shoppers pay about 99p (of which the grower gets 10p to 15p) in supermarkets. That compares with 35p for **glossy**, 'conventionally grown' carrots. Transport costs and packaging are to blame.

The Sunday Telegraph

Cut out unfair competition

Small farmers face a brick wall of government subsidies that distort competition, and facilitate a barrage of producers with their cheap imports. As taxpayers, we all **foot the bill** for roads, rail links, aviation fuel and research that make long-distance production and supply possible. Drop the subsidies, and small organic producers like myself, will take on the 'big five' supermarkets by offering better, cheaper food. Their genetically altered produce would be absurdly expensive compared with our fresh, pure, home-grown food.

The Weekend Telegraph

Rhone-Poulenc goes organic

Rhone-Poulenc, the French chemicals company, is the most unlikely **organic** farmer. Lester Noble, who manages its farm at Ongar, Essex, catalogues a familiar tale of woe. 'We've had a lot of trouble with **slugs** and also with **mildew** and septoria and a bit of nitrogen deficiency.' Rhone-Poulenc's aim was neither to knock **organic** farming nor appease the green lobby. 'There has been very little scientifically based research into the merits of **organic** food. We may find something to our advantage.'

The Sunday Telegraph

Plants defend themselves

A plant's defence mechanisms can be improved by not planting it just anywhere. Plant rotation – planting **leeks** after carrots because carrot flies do not like the smell of leeks – can be most effective. It is important to position plants which help each other, such as sweet corn and **runner beans,** next to each other. There are also certain vegetable and mineral-based solutions which make plants more resistant (**stinging nettle** compost…)

L'Indispensable

Red flag for green spray

Bacterial **spores** sprayed on **organic crops** as a pesticide may damage the health of people who inadvertantly breathe them in. French researchers have found that inhaling the **spores** can cause lung inflammation, internal bleeding and death in laboratory mice.

New Scientist

EXTRA!!! CLASSI-FILES EXTRA!!!

THÈME

1. L'agriculture **biologique** est en effet une agriculture qui nécessite beaucoup de main d'œuvre. De plus, elle est moins intensive que l'agriculture moderne et demande plus de temps et d'espace, pour des **rendements** inférieurs de 30%.
2. C'est une agriculture exempte d'**engrais** chimiques, de pesticides ou d'herbicides de synthèse, basée sur le respect des saisons et des écosystèmes. Les sols sont fertilisés avec des **engrais** naturels (fumier, débris végétaux) et au lieu d'utiliser des pesticides, les **mauvaises herbes** sont arrachées à la main.
3. C'est quand on a commencé à détruire les prédateurs naturels qu'on a eu besoin de produits chimiques pour les remplacer. Pour lutter contre les parasites, l'agriculteur utilise des insectes prédateurs, tels que la **coccinelle** qui se nourrit de **pucerons**.
4. Dans l'agriculture **biologique**, on respecte un principe de précaution face à des aliments à risques comme le sont la viande bovine ou les produits transgéniques. Les agriculteurs **biologiques** qui cultivent des terres à proximité de champs où l'on expérimente la culture transgénique, sont fort préoccupés par les risques de pollinisation croisée.
5. Longtemps perçue comme une pratique utopique de quelques **"allumés"** en mal de nature, il a fallu montrer que l'agriculture biologique pouvait être une alternative à la pratique agricole conventionnelle qui, du reste, a su produire en quantité (des produits alimentaires certes, mais aussi des **déchets** et déséquilibres de tous ordres).
6. Un **produit diététique** est créé pour répondre à des besoins nutritionnels spécifiques, dans le cas de **régimes alimentaires**. Il n'est pas forcément **bio**.

EXTRA!!! CLASSI-FILES EXTRA!!!

VERSION

1. Dedicated organic farmers complain that 'conventional' farmers, with guaranteed prices, are paid to '**set aside**' land to reduce over-production. Why not encourage them to switch to organic farming, with subsidies during the unprofitable two-year conversion period?
2. Organic fruit and vegetables compete badly with **glossy**, cheaper, intensively farmed competition. There is only so much the customer will accept.
3. Last year, French scientists isolated a **strain** of Bt that destroyed tissue in the **wounds** of a French soldier in Bosnia. Now the same team has found that H34 can kill mice with intact immune systems if they inhale the spores.
4. Organic **cattle breeders** rarely use antibiotics on their animals to avoid transferring resistance to humans, making the use of antibiotics in human medicine less effective.
5. Children are inoculated and protected by the latest pharmaceuticals, so why not the animals they eat?
6. Today's organic food comes from Morocco, Israel, Argentina, Spain and the U.S.A. Gas-guzzling planes, ships and lorries destroy and pollute our environment to bring us so-called healthy organic food.
7. Nobody can deny that Mother Nature had everything beautifully organised before man started to interfere.

1. Organic farming is indeed labour-intensive. Moreover, it is less intensive than modern agriculture; more time and space is required for a 30% lower yield.
2. It is farming based on the respect of the seasons and the ecosystem and which is free from fertilizers, pesticides and artificial weed-killer. The soil is fertilized using natural fertilizer (manure, vegetable waste). Instead of using weed-killer, the weeds are pulled out by hand.
3. We did not need chemical products to replace natural predators until we started to destroy the latter. The farmer uses predatory insects such as ladybirds which live on aphids, to combat parasites.
4. In organic farming, a cautious attitude is adopted towards risky foodstuffs such as beef or genetically modified products. Organic growers farming land near fields of experimental engineered crops, are extremely worried about the risk of cross-pollination.
5. Organic farming, which was perceived for a long time as the utopian practice of a few nature-loving loonies, has had to show it could be an alternative to traditional farming which, besides, has managed to produce a great deal (foodstuffs of course, but also waste products and all sorts of imbalances).
6. Health-foods are created in answer to some specific dietary requirement as part of a diet. They are not necessarily organic.

1. Les agriculteurs bios consciencieux se plaignent que les agriculteurs traditionnels, bénéficiant de prix garantis, sont payés pour mettre en jachère des terres, afin de réduire la surproduction. Pourquoi ne pas encourager ces derniers à passer à l'agriculture biologique, grâce à des subventions versées pendant les deux années non-rentables de la période de conversion.
2. Les fruits et légumes biologiques supportent mal la concurrence avec ceux vernissés et produits à moindre coût, de manière intensive. Il y a des limites à ce que le client est prêt à accepter.
3. L'année dernière, des scientifiques français ont réussi à isoler une souche de Bt qui a détruit des tissus sur les plaies d'un soldat français en Bosnie. Maintenant la même équipe a découvert que le H34 peut tuer des souris au système immunitaire intact si elles respirent les spores.
4. Les éleveurs de bétail biologique n'utilisent que rarement des antibiotiques sur leurs animaux pour éviter que la résistance ne soit transférée aux êtres humains, ce qui rendrait leur emploi dans la médecine humaine moins efficace.
5. Les enfants sont vaccinés et protégés par des produits pharmaceutiques dernier cri, alors pourquoi pas les animaux qu'ils mangent ?
6. La nourriture biologique d'aujourd'hui vient du Maroc, d'Israël, d'Argentine, d'Espagne et des États-Unis. Des avions, des navires et des camions qui consomment énormément d'essence, détruisent et polluent notre environnement afin de nous apporter une soi-disant nourriture biologique saine.
7. Il est indiscutable que Dame Nature avait tout bien organisé avant que l'homme ne commence à s'en mêler.

VOCABULARY

animal welfare lobby .... *défenseurs des droits des animaux*
aphid, greenfly .... *puceron*
battery hen .... *poule de batterie*
cattle breeder .... *éleveur de bétail*
C.J.D. .... *la maladie de Creutzfeldt-Jakob*
crop .... *culture, récolte, produit agricole*
dairy produce .... *produits laitiers*
diet .... *régime alimentaire*
ensure (to) .... *s'assurer*
feed .... *alimentation, fourrage*
fertiliser, fertilizer .... *engrais*
flavour .... *goût, saveur*
foot the bill (to) .... *payer l'addition*
forage (to) .... *picorer*
fossil fuel .... *combustible fossile*
fuel (to) .... *alimenter*
glossy .... *vernissé, brillant*
health food .... *produit diététique*
hold to ransom (to) .... *prendre en otage*
housekeeping bills .... *frais d'entretien du ménage*
ladybird .... *coccinelle*
lb, a pound .... *453,6 grams, une livre*
leek .... *poireau*
linger (to) .... *rester, subsister*
livestock .... *bétail*
marshes .... *marais, marécages*
mildew .... *rouille, mildiou*
loonies .... *allumés, cinglés*
organic .... *biologique*
outstrip (to) .... *devancer*
poultry .... *volaille*
rear (to) .... *élever*
riddled with .... *infesté de*
roam (to) .... *parcourir, errer*
runner beans .... *haricots verts, à rames*
scheme .... *projet, système*
set aside (to) .... *mettre en jachère*
slug .... *limace*
soar (to) .... *monter en flèche*
soil .... *terre, sol*
stinging, nettles .... *orties*
stumbling block .... *pierre d'achoppement*
strain .... *souche*
upshot .... *résultat*
waste products .... *déchets*
watchdog .... *(comité) de vigilance, gardien*
weeds .... *mauvaises herbes*
wheat .... *blé*
wound .... *plaie, blessure*
yield .... *rendement*

The arguments for and against organic food and organic farming

FOR

Consumer choice
- Organic produce tastes much better than non-organic produce.
- Consumers **are held to ransom** by the big five (five supermarket chains which dominate the market) which sell more than 70% of what we eat. Prices and **crop** choices are dictated on the basis of profit rather than in the interest of the consumer.
- The myth that people demand pristine, **soil**-free produce can be quashed by visiting farmers markets. People know that vegetables with the **soil** left on stay fresh longer.

Environment-friendly
- Centralised, intensive production and the transport of food over vast distances mean more burned **fossil fuels** and more carbon emissions. Small-scale **organic** farms delivering to the local community avoid this.

Health
- Fewer toxic chemicals in our food and in our fields will improve our health and that of the flora and fauna.
- More and more children suffer from allergies to the additives we put in our food.
- The sperm count of infertile men has been greatly improved by an **organic diet**.

Animal Welfare
- A civilised society can no longer tolerate the inhumane treatment of animals that are pumped full of chemicals to make them fatter.

AGAINST

Customer choice
- Why should customers be forced to eat mud-caked, misshapen vegetables when thanks to modern technology, we are capable of producing nice, clean, safe produce?

Animal Welfare
- Antibiotics promote the welfare of **livestock** and undertreating animals will lead to disease and suffering. Moreover there is no evidence of a link between the antibiotics in animals and human resistance to antibiotics.

Cost
- Organic food is a luxury most people cannot afford. **Housekeeping bills** would go up by about 50%.

Environmental impact
- Much more land is needed to produce the same amount of, say, **wheat**. This need for land would lead to the draining of **marshes**, the cutting down of hedges etc. for farmland.

The health issue
- It's downright dangerous not to use pesticides. Carrots can be **riddled with** disease such as carrot fly larvae. A potato contains over one hundred and fifty chemicals naturally. At least artificial chemicals are closely monitored and tightly regulated.

FREE ACCESS TO GUN

LES ARMES EN VENTE LIBRE

FACTSHEET

Confronted with the difficult issue of **guns**, the U.S.A. is almost the only developed country where all kinds of **weapons** such as **rifles**, **handguns** or **semi-automatic guns** can easily be bought without restrictions. This is why in 1998 Americans owned 235 million guns, 67 million handguns and about 40% households possessed at least one **firearm**. Americans live with them as they live with computers or household appliances and millions believe that the availability of guns must not be limited. In Britain, on the other hand, there are approximately 450,000 guns in circulation and this country has one of the most **stringent** legislation on guns in the world. A few other figures tend to prove that the gun culture is deeply enshrined within the American mentalities:

- 74% Americans oppose a total **ban** on handguns.
- 24 states do not require any **licensing** or **waiting period** before buying a handgun.
- the **NRA** with three million members and a $80 million budget is a powerful lobby.
- 31 states allow their citizens to carry **concealed weapons.**
- But the firearm-related death rate among American children under 15 was nearly 16 times higher than in 25 other industrialized countries.

Why do Americans seem to love their guns so much? *Historical reasons* may be put forward: the USA was founded by pioneers who used their guns to defend themselves against Indians, wild animals and other pioneers. The myth of the Wild West has made the gun a symbol of virility for generations of American males. Besides Hollywood films have been a wonderful propaganda machine with their cowboys, cops and war heroes who all succeed with their **mastering** of their firearm. Hence the number of people in the Western states who **carry a gun** or go to a **shooting range** to practise their sport.

Secondly the *economic aspect* should not be underplayed as many **gun makers** are American and therefore need to sell their products. Every year, Americans buy 12 million more guns and teenagers are now the new **target** of the gun industry.

Another major argument is the staunch American *individualism* which pushes them to protect themselves and their property from criminals who sometimes are '**trigger-happy**' and do not hesitate to **shoot**.

However would so many people have been shot dead – among them, famous ones like Abraham Lincoln, John and Robert Kennedy, Martin Luther King – if guns had not been so easy to possess?

Of course some **Gun Control** Acts have been passed in 1968 and 1994 yet their implementation is not satisfactory especially in Western states which are traditionally more lax about **gun control**, that is why a new way of fighting the gun lobby is to take the **gun makers** to court.

So is the free access to guns the best means to curb violent crime or is it an aggravating factor in the death of innocent people?

Guns in the Courtroom

In a New York city suit against 60 **gunmakers** and **gun sellers**, survivors of victims of gun violence are charging companies with distributing weapons in a way calculated to evade **gun-control** laws... The families of two people killed in the Jonesboro, Ark., school massacre are preparing a lawsuit against a gunmaker for not including a **trigger lock**.

Time

Freedom to shoot

The South of the USA has higher rates of gun ownership than any other region, and many here view the freedom to hunt, **shoot**, or merely collect **firearms** as a basic human right. While most gun-owners are mature, reponsible individuals, every segment of society – including those with **rifles** – has its careless, hotheaded, or even deranged members.

U.S. News & World Report

Childproofing Guns

The technology to make guns safer is available; a few gun companies have added some of those devices, like key-operated internal locks or **'loaded-chamber indicators'**, which show whether a gun is **loaded** through a colour-coded display. Such features might have prevented 31% of the 1,501 accidental shooting deaths in an earlier year. **Gun safety advocates** further argue that **firearms** should be 'personalized' so only authorized users can operate them, through use of technology that permits the gun to **fire** solely when held by someone wearing a special identifier.

U.S. News & World Report

Should kids hunt?

Mckenzie Whitmer, 12, whispers to her father: 'Can I take the **safety** off now?'. He nods; she readies her 20-**gauge** Remington **shotgun**, just the way the California department of fish and game taught her in the 10 hours of training required to get her junior **license**. [...] A pheasant takes to the air. Mckenzie tracks him with her gun **barrel**. She squeezes the **trigger**. The bird crumples, hit cleanly.

Time

The British response

The argument that the prohibition of **handguns** will penalise the **law-abiding** without having any effect on the lawless is superficial and unconvincing. Professional criminals, in Britain at least, seldom **carry** or **use firearms**. [...] but as the Dunblane, Hungerford or Tasmanian killings have shown only too vividly, it is the deranged or the disaffected who pose the threat of random **shootings** with multiple victims.

The Times

Who should carry a gun?

Is a gun-carrying nation a safer nation? Fearful of being victimized by indiscriminate violence, many Americans are gnawed by a dilemma: Should I or shouldn't I **carry a gun**? The question is a real one for a growing number of Americans because the tally of states with 'right to carry' laws has gone from eight to 31 since 1985. These states will issue a **concealed-weapon** permit to any citizen without a **criminal record** who wants one – no questions asked.

Time

EXTRA!!! CLASSI-FILES EXTRA!!!

THÈME

1. Quinze fabricants d'armes des États-Unis sont responsables de fusillades à New York, a estimé un jury fédéral qui a accordé 4 millions de dollars aux victimes. Selon le jury, la négligence des fabricants dans la distribution de leurs produits avait alimenté un marché illégal qui a permis aux criminels de se procurer des armes à feu.
2. Le drame de Littleton n'a pas manqué de relancer le débat perpétuel entre la puissante Association Nationale des Armes à Feu et les militants pour le contrôle de ces armes.
3. L'opération d'échange "armes contre jouets", lancée dans un quartier de New York a rencontré un vif succès. En quatre jours, 317 armes – fusils, pistolets, revolvers et pistolets-mitrailleurs, et même une mitrailleuse – ont été apportées par leurs propriétaires légitimes et échangées contre des bons d'achat dans une grande chaîne de jouets.
4. Les autorités judiciaires américaines envisagent à court terme de rendre plus difficile l'octroi de la "licence fédérale de vendeur d'armes", disponible actuellement pour 30 dollars à tout citoyen n'ayant pas de casier judiciaire, et qui permet à son détenteur d'acheter ou de vendre des armes d'un État à l'autre du pays – ou même par correspondance.
5. Le fait que la possession des armes à feu soit toujours inscrite dans la Constitution et que ce fait reste une valeur culturelle américaine contribue sans l'ombre d'un doute à la violence.

EXTRA!!! CLASSI-FILES EXTRA!!!

VERSION

1. The **Gun Control** Act of 1968 **banned mail-order gun sales** and regulated the interstate transportation of firearms but also produced the largest spike in gun sales recorded in American history.
2. After Congress passed the Brady Bill, mandating a five-day **waiting period** on **handgun** sales to enable **background checks**, **gunshops** saw their business jump dramatically. **Semi-automatic weapons** with large **magazines** are selling especially fast.
3. The parents of Dunblane pledged to continue their fight to have all handguns **banned** after the government announced the most **drastic** firearm curbs yet in response to the massacre of 16 children and their teacher.
4. Some **gun-rights activists** say the Littleton **shootings** bolster the case for **carrying concealed weapons**. If adults at Columbine High School had had guns nearby, the murderers might have been stopped.
5. Three fundamental rules for **gun safety** handling: always keep the gun pointed in a safe direction, always keep your finger off the **trigger** until ready to **shoot**, always keep the gun **unloaded** until ready to use.
6. A non-resident may possess a **rifle** or a **shotgun** in Massachusetts while hunting (and in possession of a valid **hunting license**), while on a **shooting range** and while travelling in Massachusetts if the rifle or shotgun is **unloaded** and enclosed in a case.

1. A federal court estimated that fifteen American gunmakers were responsible for shootings in New York and granted the victims $4 million. According to the jury, the negligence of the gun manufacturers in the distribution of their products had supplied an illegal market which enabled the criminals to get firearms.
2. The Littleton shooting is bound to start again the everlasting debate between the powerful National Rifle Association and the gun control activists.
3. The gun buy-back programme, 'guns for toys', launched in a New York suburb was a very successful one. Within four days, 317 weapons – shotguns, pistols, revolvers and semi-automatic guns and even a machine gun – were brought by their legal owners and exchanged for vouchers in a toy chain store.
4. In the short run, the American judicial authorities contemplate to make it harder to obtain the 'federal gun seller's license', now available for $30 to any citizen who has no criminal record, and which allows its holder to purchase or sell weapons in any state across the country or even by mail order.
5. What undoubtedly contributes to violence is the possession of a firearm as it still is one of the Constitutional rights and as it remains an American cultural value.

1. La Loi sur la limitation des armes à feu de 1968 a interdit la vente d'armes par correspondance et a régulé le transport des armes à feu entre États mais elle a aussi entraîné des ventes d'armes record comme les États-Unis n'en avaient jamais connu dans leur histoire.
2. Après le vote au Congrès de la Loi Brady qui impose un délai de cinq jours lors de la vente d'une arme de poing afin de permettre la vérification des antécédents, les armuriers ont vu leurs affaires progresser de manière extraordinaire. Ce sont surtout les armes semi-automatiques avec de grands chargeurs qui se sont vendues rapidement.
3. Les parents de Dunblane se sont engagés à poursuivre leur lutte pour obtenir l'interdiction de toutes les armes de poing après l'annonce faite par le gouvernement, en réponse au massacre de 16 enfants et de leur institutrice, de réduire de façon draconienne et jamais égalée le nombre d'armes à feu.
4. Certains partisans du lobby des armes disent que le massacre de Littleton justifie le droit de porter une arme cachée. Si des adultes au lycée Columbine avaient eu des armes à proximité, ils auraient pu neutraliser les meurtriers.
5. Trois règles fondamentales pour un maniement des armes en toute sécurité : pointez toujours l'arme dans une direction où il n'y a aucun risque, enlevez toujours votre doigt de la gâchette jusqu'à ce que vous soyez prêts à tirer, ne gardez jamais l'arme chargée sauf lorsque vous êtes prêts à l'utiliser.
6. Une personne qui ne réside pas au Massachusetts a le droit de posséder une carabine ou un fusil dans cet État pour la pratique de la chasse (si elle possède un permis de chasse en cours de validité), pour la pratique du tir sportif et lorsqu'elle voyage dans le Massachusetts à condition que la carabine ou le fusil soit déchargé et dans son étui.

ammunition	*munitions*
assault weapon	*fusil d'assaut*
background check	*vérification des antécédents*
ban (to)/ outlaw guns (to)	*interdire/proscrire les armes*
a ban on	*une interdiction*
barrel	*canon*
be trigger-happy (to)	*avoir la gâchette facile*
bullet	*balle*
buy a gun on the black market (to)	*acheter une arme au marché noir*
carry a concealed weapon (to)	*porter une arme dissimulée sur soi*
carry a gun (to)	*porter une arme*
deterrent	*moyen de dissuasion*
firearm	*arme à feu*
gauge	*calibre*
gun control	*limitation des armes à feu*
gun-control advocate/lobbyist	*partisan de la limitation des armes à feu*
gun laws	*législation sur les armes à feu*
gun makers	*fabricants d'armes*
gun sale	*vente d'armes*
gunshot	*coup de feu*
gun store/gunshop	*armurerie*
handgun/pistol	*arme de poing/pistolet*
handle a gun safely (to)	*manier une arme sans risque*
a hunting license	*un permis de chasse*
impose a waiting period (to)	*imposer un délai avant l'achat d'une arme*
law-abiding citizen	*citoyen respectueux de la loi*
licensing	*enregistrement*
loaded chamber indicator	*indicateur de chargement d'une balle dans la chambre*
loaded/unloaded gun	*arme chargée/déchargée*
magazine	*chargeur*
mail-order gun sale	*vente d'armes par correspondance*
master the use of a gun (to)	*maîtriser le maniement d'une arme*
the NRA (National Rifle Association)	*Association des Détenteurs d'Armes à Feu*
own a gun (to)	*posséder une arme*
pro-gun activists	*partisans du libre accès aux armes à feu*
a rifle	*carabine de chasse (à canon rayé)*
right to bear arms	*droit de porter une arme*
right-to-carry law	*loi autorisant le port d'arme*
safety lock	*verrou de sureté*
a semiautomatic weapon	*une arme semi-automatique*
shoot (to), fire (to)	*tirer*
shooting range	*stand de tir*
shotgun	*fusil de chasse (à canon lisse)*
stringent, drastic	*strict, rigoureux*
target	*cible*
trigger lock	*verrou de gâchette*
a triggerman	*homme à la gâchette facile*
use a gun (to)	*se servir d'une arme*
weapon	*arme*

The arguments for or against the free access to guns

FOR

■ According to the Second Amendment to the U.S. Constitution, 'The right of the people to keep and **bear arms** shall not be infringed' therefore any citizen should be able to use this **inalienable right** to protect himself and his family as well as his liberty.

■ The **NRA** claims that 'guns don't kill, people do' so if **firearms** are **handled safely** the shooters do not run any risks. The goals of the NRA safety programmes are to teach how to **use a gun safely** and effectively with the right ammunition.

■ **Law-abiding citizens** must be able to defend themselves in their homes as well as in the streets and guns are the best **deterrent** against criminals especially if people have the right to **carry concealed weapons**. So guns increase safety...

■ If strict **gun-control laws** are passed, many jobs will be put at risk in the gun industry as well as in the gunshops. This is why the U.S.A. blocks any move to restrict the production and the sale of light **weapons** throughout the world too.

■ Target shooting, collecting or hunting are hobbies which require the **mastering** of a **rifle**, a **shot-gun** or a **handgun** so anyone should be allowed to keep his firearm at home.

AGAINST

■ A few figures may prove what the toll paid by Americans to **firearms** is:
- In 1995, 109 people under 19 were killed by firearms in France, 19 in Britain, 57 in Germany and *5280 in the U.S.A.*
- in 1995, *35,957* Americans were killed with firearms, in homicides, suicides and accidents. In comparison, 33,651 Americans were killed in the Korean War.
- In 1996, **handguns** were used to murder 15 people in Japan, 30 in Britain, 213 in Germany and *9,390* in the United States.
- Guns kept in the home for self-protection are 43 times more likely to kill a family member or friend than to kill in self-defence.
  The question raised by those figures is: would there be so many casualties if guns were not so easily available in most states?

■ **Gun control advocates** also contend that a very high percentage of legally-bought guns are getting into the criminal market very quickly because in 30 states a private citizen is free to sell his gun to anyone.

■ Since implementation of the Brady Law in 1994 which allows officials to make sure the purchaser is qualified to **own a handgun**, there has been a significant *drop* in the number of violent crimes committed with a firearm.

■ **Gun-control lobbyists** require child **safety locks** on all guns to avoid accidents, '**load indicator**' to indicate if there is a **bullet** in the **chamber** of the handgun. They argue that firearms should be 'personalized' so only the user who wears a special bracelet with a computer chip may **fire** the gun. Most countries have some restrictions on firearms and fewer school shootings, fewer gun-related homicides and accidents so shouldn't the U.S.A. try to launch a more sensible gun policy?

GOD SAVE THE QUEEN?

LA MONARCHIE, POURQUOI ?

FACTSHEET

The british head of state is queen Elizabeth II. She has several vital roles, including Head of the Executive, Head of the Judiciary, Commander-in-Chief of the Armed Forces and Supreme Governor of the Church of England.

'The Queen reigns but doesn't **rule**':

– she officially **appoints** the **Prime Minister**, but she actually always chooses the leader of the party which has obtained a majority in the **House of Commons** after **a general election**.

– As 'Fountain of Honour', the Monarch is able to confer peerages, **knighthoods** and other honours; she also appoints important officials such as senior **civil servants**, **senior** members of the Judiciary (the British Monarch is the 'Fountain of Justice'); but, when doing so, the Queen always acts on the advice and recommendations she receives from the Prime Minister or from Government Ministers.

Her other roles include summoning, proroguing and dissolving Parliament, and giving the **Royal Assent** to **bills** voted by the two Houses of Parliament. At the State Opening of Parliament, she delivers the '**Speech from the Throne**', or Queen's Speech, announcing 'her' government's legislative plans for the coming session.

The Monarch, who is the 'Defender of the Faith', has to be a member of the Church of England ('Whosoever shall hereafter come to the possession of this crown shall joyn in communion with the Chuch of England as by law established.' The **Act** of Settlement.1701)

The Monarch and royal **household** expenses are covered by the Civil List (about £8M a year), an annual subsidy which is voted by Parliament.

Queen Elizabeth was born on April 21, 1926. At birth, she stood third in line to the throne after her uncle Edward (later Edward VIII who abdicated in 1936, as he wished to marry a divorcee) and her father who became George VI.

She married Prince Philip in 1947. Their first child, Charles, was born in 1948, followed by Anne in 1950, Andrew in 1960 and Edward in 1964.

She was crowned at Westminster Abbey in 1953. She is the fortieth monarch since William the Conqueror; she is already the sixth longest reigning monarch since 1066.

> This system prevents politicians from too easily usurping power and, it may be argued, has prevented a dictator from dominating Great Britain since Oliver Cromwell's short **rule** in the 17th century.
> It is one of the great strengths of monarchy that it has never **taken sides** in any political debate, that it shows itself, as an institution, to be **even-handed**. This apolitical **stance** has made it possible for the political culture of Great Britain to assimilate, with relative ease, theories that would appear on the face of things to be radically at odds with a system of monarchical government.
>
> *Newsweek*

Britain needs a head of state in possession of reserve powers to check and balance the government. The Economist would rather that this were an elected president on the German model, with the monarchy abolished. But if the monarchy is to be retained, it must surely retain its reserve powers and its constitutional role. Hold referendums for its successions and disestablish the church by all means. But the House of Windsor has to keep an eye on its core competence: being born, being non-political, and simply being there.

The Economist

There is little doubt that much of the Church of England would find it unacceptable that the Church's supreme governor would be a remarried divorcé. It is no doubt true that the Church could not stop it happening, and that public opinion would find it supportable. The Established Church however would be badly divided: fundamentalists might refuse to accept Prince Charles as head of their Church. And the case for disestablishment would be revived.

The Guardian

For the first time, an **opinion poll** has indicated that more than half of the British people believe Prince William should succeed to the throne in place of his father. The number believing that the throne should 'skip a generation' is now 51%.

The Daily Telegraph

Too many republicans think it is enough to cry 'anachronism' or 'indefensible hereditary privilege', and that the argument will be won. That might be the case if the monarchy were being set up today from scratch. But it is not. The emotional case for keeping such a long-established institution is a strong one: it is a link to tradition and history, and is a powerful **trademark** for Britain. Some love it deeply whatever the foibles of the present royal family. Others, perhaps the largest group of all, feel less strongly, but think of it rather as they might an old building: it may not be very practical, but they like the look of it.

The Economist

In the past, republican feeling would be mediated through the London mob and royalist support nurtured by ceremony and sacrament. Now, republican sentiment has been fed by scandal and encouraged by political activists who see in constitutional reform an outlet for the energies which might once have been directed to banning the bomb or saving the whale.

The Times

THÈME

1. Dans la pratique, le choix du Premier Ministre est automatique : la Reine nomme le chef du parti qui détient une majorité à la Chambre des communes.
2. La monarchie a survécu parce qu'elle rappelle aux Britanniques que la nation existe et que l'institution s'inscrit dans une perspective historique.
3. La continuité de la monarchie est contestée ; il faut que les Windsor opèrent un changement radical s'ils veulent préserver l'institution.
4. Les Britanniques ne parvenaient pas à s'affranchir de leur souvenir d'un passé impérial avec ses traditions et son protocole "vieux jeu"; la mort de Diana les a peut-être aidés à rompre avec ce passé.
5. Les mésaventures de la famille royale, exploitées par la presse populaire, ont exacerbé les griefs de l'anglais moyen à l'égard des Windsor.
6. Le contribuable supporte de plus en plus mal de subvenir aux besoins de la famille royale, même si, depuis 1992, la Reine accepte de payer un impôt sur le revenu.

VERSION

1. The simple, straightforward case against monarchy is that in a democracy it is inappropriate for the head of state to be determined by heredity. Positions of public authority should, wherever possible, be acquired on merit and confirmed by a democratic mandate.
2. If there is ever to be any change in Britain's method of choosing its head of state, the **burden of proof** in justifying such a change **lies with** the republicans, not with the monarchists.
3. This **opinion poll** shows the only age group that believes Britain would be worse off without the royals is the over-65s.
4. Seeing the public's apparently insatiable appetite for insider **gossip**, the **tabloid press** realized it had a lucrative franchise and began turning the visibility into voyeurism; meanwhile, the palace stuck to old practices, declining to comment on rumours and refusing to **sue** for **libel**.
5. Stung by criticism that the monarchy had appeared aloof following the princess's death, the Queen **paid tribute** to the Princess of Wales on the eve of her funeral in an unprecedented television and radio address to the nation.
6. On November 14th, the 50th birthday of Prince Charles will cast a spotlight on the most audacious **rebranding** yet attempted: the attempt to transform the image of the **heir** to the throne.
7. If Prince Charles harbours the twin ambitions of becoming king and marrying the woman he loves, his **spin-doctors** still have some work to do.

1. In practice, the choice of the **Prime Minister** is automatic: the Queen appoints the leader of the majority party in the **House of Commons.**
2. Monarchy has survived, for it reminds British people that their nation exists in a historical perspective in which the institution fits.
3. The continuity of the Monarchy is openly **challenged**; the House of Windsor has to change radically if they want to maintain the institution.
4. The British couln't shake off the remembrance of an imperial past with its traditions and its stuffy protocol; the death of Diana may have helped them break with the past.
5. The misfortune of the royal family, exploited by the **tabloid press**, has aggravated the average citizen's resentment against the Windsors.
6. The **taxpayer** is more and more reluctant to subsidize the royal family, even if, since1992, the Queen has agreed to pay **income tax**.

1. Il y a un argument simple et clair qui s'oppose à la monarchie, c'est qu'il ne convient pas, dans une démocratie, que la légitimité du chef de l'état soit dictée par l'hérédité. Chaque fois que cela est possible, les charges publiques devraient être conférées selon le mérite et entérinées par un mandat démocratique.
2. S'il doit y avoir en Grande-Bretagne un changement dans la procédure de désignation du chef de lÉtat, la charge de la preuve permettant de justifier un tel changement incombe aux partisans de la république, non à la monarchie.
3. Ce sondage montre que la seule tranche d'âge qui estime que la Grande-Bretagne serait plus mal en point s'il n'y avait plus de famille royal est celle des plus de 65 ans.
4. Devant l'appétit apparemment insatiable du public pour les potins puisés à bonne source, la presse populaire a compris qu'elle disposait d'une franchise rentable et a commencé de confondre transparence et voyeurisme. Pendant ce temps, Buckingham Palace, qui s'en tenait aux usages anciens, se refusait à commenter les rumeurs ou à intenter des procès en diffamation.
5. Piquée au vif par les critiques qui, à la suite de la mort de la Princesse Diana, avaient trouvé la monarchie distante, la Reine a rendu hommage à la Princesse de Galles à la veille de ses obsèques, à l'occasion d'une intervention sans précédent à la radio et à la télévision.
6. Le 50e anniversaire du Prince Charles, le 14 novembre, sera l'occasion d'un coup de projecteur sur ce qui est jusqu'à ce jour la plus audacieuse entreprise de redéfinition d'image : la transformation de celle de l'héritier du trône.
7. Si le Prince Charles nourrit la double ambition d'accéder au trône tout en épousant la femme qu'il aime, ses conseillers en communication ont encore du pain sur la planche.

VOCABULARY

Act of Parliament	*loi votée par le Parlement*
agenda	*ordre du jour, programme*
appoint (to)	*désigner*
bill	*projet de loi*
burden of proof	*charge de la preuve*
challenge (to)	*contester, récuser*
check (to)	*contrôler*
civil servant	*fonctionnaire*
core	*noyau ; partie essentielle*
Established Church	*Église Établie*
even-handed	*impartial*
general election	*élections législatives*
gossip	*commérage ; potin*
heir	*héritier*
household	*maison (ici, maison royale)*
House of Commons	*chambre des communes*
income tax	*impôt sur le revenu*
inherit (to)	*hériter*
irrelevant	*hors de propos*
knighthood	*titre de chevalier*
libel	*diffamation (sous forme d'écrit)*
lie with (to)	*incomber*
opinion poll	*sondage*
pay tribute (to)	*rendre hommage*
Prime Minister	*Premier ministre*
rebranding	*redéfinition d'image (communication, publicité)*
Royal Assent	*accord du souverain (à la loi votée au parlement)*
rule (to)	*gouverner ; gouvernement, autorité*
senior	*de grade supérieur*
Speech from the Throne	*"discours du trône"*
spin-doctor	*conseiller en communication*
stance	*position, attitude*
sue (to)	*poursuivre en justice*
tabloid press	*presse populaire*
take sides (to)	*prendre parti*
taxpayer	*contribuable*
trademark	*marque (de fabrique)*
undermine (to)	*ébranler, saper*

FOR

- Monarchy has remained a unifying national symbol; as a long standing institution, it provides continuity.
- Popular support may have dropped and some members of the royal family are resented; not all, though: asked to choose between different candidates for an elected president, the interviewees for an **opinion poll** placed Princess Anne, the Queen's daughter, ahead of 12 other key figures.
- As long as Britain doesn't have a written constitution, or a Bill of Rights, the sovereign may appear to be the protector of basic human rights and of the institutions.
- A clear majority of British people still wish the monarchy to survive.
- It is hard to discover a strong movement toward a republic; no political party argues for ending the monarchy, as they reckon any attack might lead to the loss of potential support for the rest of their political **agenda**.
- Shouldn't a reform of the monarchy be part of a vast reform of the British institutions targeting for instance the House of Lords or the electoral system?
- Monarchy is at the centre of a huge tourist industry; it boosts the nation's commerce.

AGAINST

- There is no rational justification for hereditary public offices, for a hereditary head of state. A democrat will always favour reward for achievement rather than **inheritance**.
- Most royal prerogatives which officially **lie with** the sovereign are today exercised by the Prime Minister and his government; one of these prerogatives is to dissolve Parliament; but in practice it simply results from the application of the law (a **general election** must be held at least every five years) or from the wish of the Prime Minister himself to dissolve in anticipation and proceed to a **general election**.
- The **Speech from the Throne**, or Queen's Speech, which discloses 'Her Majesty's government 'legislative plans, is actually written by the Prime Minister and read by the monarch.
- The royal family has for a long time stuck too closely to stiff protocol and regal pomp, seeming increasingly **irrelevant**. And the royals won't reinvent themselves and **rebrand** the monarchy with easy tricks such as the Queen visiting a pub or Prince Charles posing with the Spice Girls.
- For a long time, the royal family had represented a model of virtue and tradition: the young royals' behaviour, scandals and divorces have impaired the image and **undermined** the popularity of the monarchy and darkened its future.
- Popular support has slumped; people often disapprove of royal behaviour; the British **taxpayers** resent the cost of the monarchy; a growing minority of British people believe that their country would be better off without it: then, the monarchy is no longer uniting Britain but dividing it.
- After Queen Elizabeth, will there be as strong a personality to succeed her?

ORANGEMEN *VS* PAPISTS

ORANGISTES CONTRE PAPISTES

FACTSHEET

'To Connaught or to hell!'

Oliver Cromwell is said to have pronounced, 'Let them go to Connaught or to hell!' By 'them', he meant the Irish Catholics, whom he wished to eliminate from the territory of Ireland. Indeed, the Irish Catholics were obliged to emigrate to Connaught, i.e. the West of Ireland, which was then a **barren**, inhospitable area. Their lands were confiscated and given to Scottish and English Protestant **settlers**. This policy of 'plantation' had in fact started as early as 1541. This policy of anglicizing Ireland led to severe repressions and the voting of **harsh** laws called the Penal Laws or **Popery** Code from 1695 onwards.

But the territory of Ireland had first been occupied by the Celts or Gaels. The Christianisation of the island had started in the 5th century under the efforts of a man called Patricius, coming either from Britain or France, hence Patrick's Day (17th March), the National Day in Ireland.

A Nation Divided:

– Who are the Orangemen?

The name goes back to William of Orange who reigned over Britain from 1689 till 1702, as William III. He and his troops defeated an Irish rebellion in support of King James II who had been **ousted** from his throne after trying to impose Catholicism in England. The Battle of the Boyne on Ist July 1690 is now yearly celebrated by Protestants wearing bowler hats and orange **sashes**, who organize 'marches' in July.

This battle has become a symbol of Protestant ascendancy in the eyes of **hard-liners**.

– Who are the 'Papists'?

This term is used by Protestant Unionists to refer to the Catholics. This is a **derogatory** term which sums up the **contempt** in which the Catholics have always been held by the Protestants. After the partition of Ireland in 1920, the north of the isle was called Northern Ireland and comprised six counties of the province of Ulster with Belfast as its capital. The southern half became the Irish Free State and later, in 1948, the Republic of Ireland or Eire, with Dublin as its capital. Ever since, most Catholics have regarded the province, designed from the start to make them a minority, as alien and illegitimate.

A Nation Once Again?

However, at long last, there was hope that peace might be achieved. On 31st August 1994, the **I.R.A.** declared a cease-fire, followed a few weeks later by a similar one from the Protestant paramilitaries, thus putting an end to 25 years of bombings and sectarian killings which have claimed nearly 3,500 lives. Then, in April 1998, a peace agreement, called 'the Good Friday agreement', was signed and approved in a referendum in June by the populations of both Irelands. David Trimble, a Protestant, was elected 'first minister' and leader of the Northern Ireland Assembly which will **henceforth** rule the province instead of the British. Yet, tragic events soon **marred** the **ensuing** euphoria.

From forward march to retreat

The murder of three small boys in an **arson** attack has thrown the Protestant Order into **disarray** in Northern Ireland.

The Economist

We're agreed, then

David Trimble, the leader of the Ulster Unionist Party, and Gerry Adams, president of **Sinn Féin**, both campaigned for a yes vote on the Northern Ireland peace agreement. But, despite this common cause, the two men have never spoken to each other. Trimble even refuses **to make eye contact** when their path happens to cross.

Time

Voices

'We're going down the road to a United Ireland. If that happens, civil war will come. Protestants will never **surrender**.' (Gordon Young, Security Guard, Protestant)

'We don't expect the IRA to disappear off the face of the earth. They will continue, but Sinn Fein will negotiate. (Mary Kennedy, Catholic housewife)

'Maybe we'll get back to the days when Protestants and Catholics could hate each other and just get on with life' (Alan Hunter, teacher, Protestant)

'I recognize the fears of the loyalists. We're just starting a very long process' (Máiréad Maguire, Peace activist, Catholic).

Newsweek

Attack on Peace

The bloodiest **bombing** in Ulster's violent history scores a direct hit on the Good Friday Agreement. Will the terrorists **gain the upper hand**?

Newsweek

Peace is not impossible

The **twin** demons of Northern Ireland – violence and intransigence must be overcome. Of course there are those who don't want anything to change. They want to recreate a past that is gone forever. But their way will only guarantee never-ending conflict (American Senator George Mitchell, chairman of the negotiations on the future of Northern Ireland).

Newsweek

Summer of Hatred

A **RUC** decision to **cancel** a tradional Protestant march **sparked** three days of **rioting** as Unionists across Northern Ireland protested the perceived insult to their heritage. When the march was abruptly reinstated, the Catholics exploded in anger. By Friday the tourists who were boosting the region's economy had fled, **arson fires** were burning, hundreds were injured, and the politicians were wondering how **to get** peace negotiations **back on track**.

Time

United they stand

Since the beginning of the Troubles, Londonderry has become increasingly **ghettoized**. More than 20,000 Protestants have fled the central section of the city on the west bank. So drastic was the exodus that some in the Catholic community sent Christmas cards to residents in the Fountain area, the last remaining Protestant enclave, **urging** them to stay in their homes.

Time

EXTRA!!! CLASSI-FILES EXTRA!!!

THÈME

1. Le conflit en Irlande du Nord concerne deux groupes au sein de deux communautés historiques qui vivent en Ulster depuis environ trois siècles, les protestants de souche britannique, et les catholiques de souche irlandaise. On peut dire que, fondamentalement, les populations des deux côtés n'ont jamais réussi à s'entendre.
2. Pour les nationalistes irlandais, la partition de l'Irlande reste artificielle et injuste, et constitue le fond du problème. Pour les unionistes d'Ulster, la partition n'est que le reflet de différences culturelles, religieuses, économiques et politiques en Irlande, ce que les nationalistes refusent d'accepter.
3. En juillet 1998, des centaines d'Orangistes campèrent à proximité de Garvaghy Road, située dans un quartier catholique de la petite ville de Portadown. Ils réclamaient le droit de défiler depuis l'église de Drumcree, droit que les catholiques ont toujours considéré comme une violation des leurs.
4. Le 15 août 1998, un attentat à la bombe dans la petite ville d'Omagh, attribué à un groupe de terroristes catholiques radicaux, fit près de trente morts, catholiques et protestants, de tous âges. Il était d'autant plus horrible qu'il survenait après des mois d'espoir.
5. Même si de gros progrès ont été faits, la société d'Irlande du Nord reste sectaire. On ne peut pas du jour au lendemain effacer la haine et la peur qui se sont accumulées pendant des générations.

EXTRA!!! CLASSI-FILES EXTRA!!!

VERSION

1. In April 1998, a short time after the Good Friday Agreement, the government decided to build a barrier to separate two neighbourhoods in the White City area of north Belfast, one Catholic, the other Protestant. There are many such walls in the city.
2. Says Samuel Graham, a 16-year old who wants to be a British soldier and lives in Belfast in a Protestant enclave where pro-unionists fly the Ulster **flag** from **lampposts**: 'The Catholics attack us. They want our homes.'
3. To try and **defuse** violence, Britain as well as the United States and the European Union have **poured** a lot of money into Northern Ireland in order to finance various community groups and programs, such as cross-community projects which mix Catholics and Protestants, or helping young people acquire **employment skills**.
4. One of the central figures in the **round** of negotiations has been John Hume, the leader of the Social Democratic and Labour Party. The SDLP is an Irish nationalist party, **committed to** a United Ireland through peaceful means with the consent of a majority in the North. Both he and David Trimble were awarded the Nobel Peace Prize.
5. Unionist leaders remain **suspicious** of recent developments. The more extreme Democratic Unionist Party, led by Ian Paisley, has called the British government's position **'surrender'** and even warned that the peace process could lead to civil war.

1. The conflict in Northern Ireland concerns two communities within the two historic communities which have lived in Ulster for about three centuries: the Protestants of British origin and the Catholics of Irish origin. It can be said that, basically, the populations of both sides have never succeeded in getting along together.
2. To the Irish nationalists, the partition of Ireland remains artificial and unfair and lies at the root of the problem. To the Ulster unionists, partition merely reflects cultural, religious, economic and political problems within Ireland, which the nationalists refuse to accept.
3. In July 1998, hundreds of Protestant Orangemen camped on the edge of Garvaghy Road, situated in a Catholic district of the small town of Portadown. They demanded the right to march from the Church of Drumcree, which the Catholics have always regarded as a violation of their own rights.
4. On the 15th August 1998, a bombing attack in the small town of Omagh, attributed to a group of radical Catholic terrorists, killed nearly thirty people, Catholic and Protestant, of all ages. It was all the more horrific as it came after months of hope.
5. Even though great progress has been made, the society of Northern Ireland remains sectarian. One cannot overnight eradicate the feelings of hatred and fear which have accumulated over generations.

1. En avril 1998, peu de temps après les accords de paix du Vendredi Saint, le gouvernement décida d'ériger une barrière pour séparer les deux communautés dans le quartier du White City au nord de Belfast, l'une catholique, l'autre protestante. Il y a beaucoup de murs semblables dans la ville.
2. Samuel Graham, un jeune de 16 ans qui veut être soldat britannique et qui vit dans une enclave protestante où les pro-unionistes accrochent le drapeau d'Ulster aux lampadaires, déclare : "Les catholiques nous attaquent. Ils veulent nos maisons."
3. Pour essayer de désamorcer la violence, la Grande-Bretagne ainsi que les États-Unis et l'Union Européenne ont versé beaucoup d'argent à l'Irlande du Nord dans le but de financer diverses associations et groupes communautaires, tels que des projets intercommunautaires mêlant catholiques et protestants, ou aider des jeunes à acquérir des qualifications professionnelles.
4. L'une des figures centrales dans la série de négociations a été John Hume, le chef du parti travailliste et socio-démocrate. Le SDLP est un parti nationaliste irlandais, ayant pour objectif une Irlande unifiée obtenue pacifiquement avec le consentement d'une majorité au nord. Avec David Trimble, il a reçu le prix Nobel de la Paix.
5. Les dirigeants unionistes restent méfiants à l'égard des événements récents. Le parti le plus extrême, le parti unioniste démocratique, dirigé par Ian Paisley, a qualifié de 'reddition' la position du gouvernement britannique et a même averti que le processus de paix pourrait mener à une guerre civile.

VOCABULARY

achieve (to)	*réaliser*
alleviate (to)	*soulager*
appoint (to)	*nommer (à un poste)*
arson (fire)	*incendie criminel*
award (to)	*décerner*
barren	*désertique*
bombing (attack)	*attentat à la bombe*
cancel (to)	*annuler*
committed to	*ayant pour objectif*
contempt	*mépris*
decommissioning	*démantèlement*
defuse (to)	*désamorcer*
derogatory	*désobligeant*
disarray	*confusion, désordre*
employment skills	*qualification professionnelle*
ensuing	*qui s'ensui(vi)t*
flag	*drapeau*
fledgling	*novice*
gain the upper hand (to)	*prendre le dessus*
get...back on track (to)	*reprendre le fil*
ghettoize (to)	*devenir un ghetto*
hard-liner	*inconditionnel, dur*
harsh	*dur*
hell	*enfer*
henceforth	*dorénavant*
IRA.*(Irish Republican Army)*	*organisation paramilitaire*
lamppost	*lampadaire*
make eye contact (to)	*échanger un regard*
mar (to)	*gâcher*
mood	*disposition, état d'esprit*
oust from (to)	*évincer, chasser*
overwhelming, overwhelmingly	*écrasant(e), d'une manière écrasante*
Popery	*Papisme*
pour (to)	*verser*
reinstate (to)	*rétablir*
riot, rioting	*émeute*
round	*série*
RUC	*police (de l'Irlande du Nord)*
rule (to)	*diriger*
sash	*écharpe*
settler, settlement	*colon, règlement*
shatter (to)	*briser*
Sinn Féin	*Sinn Fein (du gaélique : Nous-Mêmes ; mouvement nationaliste irlandais, branche politique de l'I.R.A.)*
spark (to)	*déclencher*
surrender	*reddition, se rendre*
suspicious	*méfiant*
twin	*jumeau*
urge (to)	*exhorter*

Is peace possible in Northern Ireland? On what conditions?

FOR: The reasons why peace is near at hand.

- The **mood** is right. People are fed up with the violence. The **overwhelming** majority of people in Northern Ireland want political stability and reconciliation.
- This would put an end to decades of hatred and sectarianism.
- It would enable Catholics to be citizens in their own rights instead of being subject to job discrimination and segregation.
- The horror and revulsion felt by both sides at the Omagh bombing has drawn the two communities closer.
- Much attention has been paid to the terms and the way in which the newly elected Northern Assembly will be run, to avoid past mistakes when similar attempts to create a Northern Ireland government had been made.
- The fears of the Protestants concerning a possible reunification of the North and the South have been **alleviated** after the Republic of Ireland modified a clause in its constitution aiming at a united Ireland.
- There is considerable pressure on the part of the United States (President Clinton paid a visit to Northern Ireland during the peace negotiations) and the European Union to find a lasting **settlement**.
- The political mentalities have changed. Instead of turning to the past and trying to recreate a united Gaelic Ireland (which in fact has never existed), the nationalist movements have come to realise that armed struggle has become anachronistic and useless.
- Everyone is now agreed on the need to generate a peace dividend and boost the economy: tourists would come to the North in great numbers; firms would be attracted by the opportunities to find cheap labour. This would help reduce the very high level of unemployment among young Catholics.

AGAINST: The problems that remain to be solved.

- The **decommissioning** of weapons. The IRA and other paramilitaries have not yet surrendered their formidable arsenal of arms and explosives. This is a very delicate issue.
- Not everybody is in favour of present-day agreements. Some, among Irish Americans for instance, want to go on fighting in order to **achieve** independence from Britain.
- The Unionists think that they will lose the political power they once enjoyed. Some extremists, such as Ian Paisley, have accused the British government of abandoning them and favouring the nationalists too much. - It is not easy to change habits overnight; Ian Paisley called George Mitchell 'the pope'.
- There is still a substantial number of Protestants who consider themselves as British subjects and not as Irish and refuse to be amalgamated into an **overwhelmingly** Catholic country, if and when reunification takes place.
- The situation remains fragile. The Northern Ireland Assembly is still a **fledgling** body.

Question pouvant servir de base à un travail en classe :

- What would be the advantages and/or drawbacks of a reunification of Ireland (from the points of view of the two communities)?

GENETIC ENGINEERING

MANIPULATIONS GÉNÉTIQUES

FACTSHEET

Genetics is the area of biology concerned with the study of heredity, that is to say the process by which certain characteristics of organisms are handed down from a parent to his/her **offspring**.

Genetic engineering is the method that scientists use to change the inherited characteristics of an organism. They alter its genetic material to obtain some specific predetermined change in the organism. **Genetic engineering** has been **effectively** practised in **animal husbandry**, horticulture, and agriculture for thousands of years through **selective breeding**. More recently, in the early eighties, the first 'sperm–banks for geniuses' were created in an attempt to apply selective breeding techniques to human beings. Thus Nobel prizewinners donated their sperm in an experiment designed to produce 'super-babies'.

Recent discoveries in molecular genetics have permitted the *direct* manipulation of the genetic material itself.

The technique used is that of **recombinant-DNA**-formation. It is a procedure whereby segments of genetic material are transferred from one organism to another.

Tinkering with DNA allows scientists to develop animals and plants with desirable properties. Bacteria, for example, can be made capable of producing human proteins, cows can be altered so that they produce milk containing **drugs**, pigs so that they produce 'humanised' organs for transplant; crops so that they produce pesticides, haemoglobin or plastic.

The medical use of **genetic engineering** is called '**gene therapy**' and it is used to implant a gene that is lacking or damaged in a **patient** in order to correct hereditary disease, for example for the treatment of cancers and blood, **liver**, and **lung** disorders.

The most famous **genetic engineering** programme is the 'Human **genome** project' which is an international effort to locate every element of the human **genetic blueprint**. The aim is to scan and decode the complete DNA sequence of any human being in order to map and eventually control the 100,000 genes which combine to produce and constitute a human being.

While the potential benefits of **genetic engineering** are considerable, one should be aware of the potential dangers, despite **stringent** controls, some unforeseen effect might occur.

Few people realise that a genetic 'land grab' is taking place on a **scale** that rivals 19th century colonialism. This time the prize is not gold and diamonds, but the unexploited gene **pools**.

Multinational corporations are spending billions of dollars each year buying up or **reaching** licensing agreements with hot biotech prospects.
On the whole we no longer speak of genetic manipulations but of **genetic engineering**, nonetheless many still view these techniques with suspicion and the fact that the popular name for the 1980 ruling by the US Supreme Court (Diamond v Chakrabarty) which stipulates that new forms of life created in the laboratory may be **patented,** is 'the Frankenstein law' is highly significant.

Research will produce a guide to the mechanics of health

Just like a car, we are full of duplication and redundancy; and many of our **components** have begun to rust, with battered copies littering the DNA. Two people out of three in the West die from reasons linked to an error in their genetic machinery.

The Daily Telegraph

Rapid advances in genetics will soon transform biological **weapons** into potent tools of **ethnic cleansing** and terrorism…

'In genetic terms there are more similarities between different people and peoples than there are differences, but the differences exist, and may, singly or in combination, distinguish the members of one social group from another. These markers could be harnessed as triggers so that an agent such as a disease-carrying virus would be **harmless** to those who did not possess them.

Genetic warfare is not, in all probability, a practical possibility today. A growing number of scientists are issuing warnings that such methods will soon be possible.

The Daily Telegraph

An ethical battle rages as prospectors scour the globe to find – and profit from – organisms that could cure some of the world's worst diseases.

It's a hunt critics call 'gene piracy'. Everybody wants a piece of the genetic mother**lode**… the contest **pits** industrialised nations against the developing world, multinational companies against ecologists and social activists, and governments against their own tribal people.

Time

Booty and the Beast

The modern Chimera **slumbers** in the **bowels** of the United States **Patent** and Trademark Office in Washington DC. Part-chimpanzee, part-pig, part-human, this monster is real – or at least it would be, should technology ever **override** morality…

Such a creature could be trained to perform **menial tasks** carried out by the less skilled members of the workforce, but without such expenses as wages or health benefits. It could be used to test experimental drugs. Or its organs could be **harvested** for human transplantation. Either way, the rights to make such a valuable commodity could make someone very rich.

The Daily Telegraph

Selling the family secrets

Iceland plans to put its people's genetic history in the hands of a single company.

A large majority of **MPs** support the **bill**, which is still being revised… they claim the deal will bring prestige to the country and create hundreds of new jobs in research. In addition, Hoffman-La Roche has agreed to supply Icelanders free of charge with any medicines that result from their research.

The New Scientist

Genetics research can improve drugs.

Within a decade, pharmacogenomics could provide effective drugs personalised to match patients' symptoms with their individual genetic make-ups.

The Daily Telegraph

THÈME

1. Des vaccins plus sûrs grâce au génie génétique.
2. Le spermatozoïde transgénique pourrait remplacer le clonage dans la fabrication du bétail transgénique.
3. La thérapie génique consiste à réparer des gènes abîmés ou à remplacer des gènes manquants.
4. Construire des pièces de rechange flambant neuves pour réparer cette machine sophistiquée qu'est le corps humain : c'est le défi du génie tissulaire, une discipline en plein essor.
5. Grâce au génie génétique on pourra bientôt créer des médicaments personnalisés.
6. Une fois que l'on a trouvé quel gène, dans l'organisme d'un malade, est défaillant, on injecte un gène en bon état qui vient pallier les carences ou les défauts du gène visé.
7. Les techniques du génie génétique permettent aux scientifiques d'identifier des gènes spécifiques, d'ôter n'importe lequel de ces gènes du chromosome d'un organisme, de le cloner ou d'en faire de nombreuses copies à l'identique. Elles permettent également d'analyser une copie en détail, de modifier le gène, et de le réintroduire soit dans le génome de l'organisme dont il a été prélevé, soit dans le génome d'un autre organisme qu'il soit similaire ou très différent.
8. Le génie génétique offrira aux scientifiques l'occasion sans précédent de façonner la race humaine.
9. Avant que des médicaments personnalisés d'un nouvel âge puissent être introduits sur le marché, il faudra résoudre le problème de la lecture précise du patrimoine génétique humain dans toute sa diversité.

VERSION

1. Some gene **rustlers** view humans as fair game. Isolated **tribes** are sought for their unique resistance or vulnerability to certain diseases.
2. If cash-poor countries start fencing off their gene **pools**, everyone will suffer. Of course multinationals want to make money, but who else is going to pour in the hundreds of millions of dollars it takes to develop new **drugs**?
3. Weapons that could distinguish between ethnic groups by exploiting tiny genetic or cellular differences could be a reality within a decade.
4. Private companies want to **patent** what useful genes they can, whereas the Human Genome Project is passionately opposed to **patents**, and **dumps** its findings on to the Internet every night in an effort to prevent them.
5. Parents pass their genes to their **offspring** and the basic characteristics of a **species** are passed down through the generations.
6. Questions have been raised by a number of scientists and **lay people** on the advisabi-lity and ethics of **recombinant DNA** research.
7. Newman and Rifkin's Chimera **patent** is intended to **foil** the growing commercial interest in genetic and biological **patents** and prevent such monsters from being created.

1. Safer vaccines thanks to genetic engineering.
2. Transgenic sperm could replace cloning in the production of transgenic cattle.
3. Gene therapy consists in repairing damaged genes or in replacing missing genes.
4. Making brand new spare parts to repair this sophisticated machine, known as the human body, is the challenge of tissue engineering, a science in full expansion.
5. Thanks to genetic engineering, it will soon be possible to create personalised drugs.
6. Once a patient's defective gene has been identified, a healthy gene is inserted so as to remedy the deficiencies or defects of the targeted gene.
7. The techniques of genetic engineering allow scientists to identify specific genes, to remove any one of these genes from an organism's chromosome, to clone or make a large number of identical copies of that gene. They also enable scientists to analyse a copy in detail, to modify the gene, and to reinsert it either into the genetic material of the organism from which it was derived or into the genetic material of a similar or very different organism.
8. Genetic engineering will offer scientists an unprecedented opportunity to mould the human race.
9. Before a new age of personalised medicine can be marketed, the problem of how to accurately read the human **genetic blueprint** in all its diversity will have to be solved.

1. Certains voleurs de gènes considèrent les humains comme une proie rêvée. Des tribus isolées sont recherchées pour leur extraordinaire résistance ou vulnérabilité à certaines maladies.
2. Si les pays pauvres se mettent à entourer d'une barrière protectrice leurs bassins de gènes, tout le monde en souffrira. Bien sûr, les multinationales veulent des profits, mais qui d'autre versera les millions de dollars indispensables au développement de nouveaux médicaments ?
3. Des armes pouvant reconnaître différents groupes ethniques en exploitant de minuscules différences génétiques ou cellulaires pourraient devenir une réalité d'ici une décennie.
4. Les compagnies privées veulent breveter autant de gènes utiles que possible tandis que le Programme pour le Génome Humain est farouchement opposé aux brevets et chaque soir inonde l'Internet de ses découvertes afin d'empêcher les brevets.
5. Les parents transmettent leurs gènes à leur progéniture et les caractéristiques fondamentales d'une espèce sont transmises de génération en génération.
6. De nombreux scientifiques et non-spécialistes soulèvent des questions quant à l'opportunité et l'éthique de la recherche sur l'ADN recombinant.
7. Le brevet de la Chimère de Newman et Rifkin vise à déjouer l'intérêt commercial grandissant pour les brevets en génétique et biologie ainsi qu'à empêcher que de tels monstres soient créés.

VOCABULARY

ageing	*vieillissement*
animal husbandry	*élevage d'animaux (agriculture)*
bill	*un projet de loi*
bowels	*entrailles*
components	*composants*
decipher (to)	*déchiffrer*
defective	*déficient*
demean (to)	*rabaisser, dégrader*
drugs	*médicaments*
dump (to)	*décharger, déverser*
effectively	*avec succès*
ethnic cleansing	*purification éthnique*
experiment	*expérience scientifique*
foil (to)	*déjouer*
gene therapy	*thérapie génique*
genetic engineering	*génie génétique*
genetic warfare	*guerre génétique*
genome, genetic make-up, genetic blueprint	*patrimoine génétique, génome*
germ line gene therapy	*thérapie génique des gamettes*
harmless	*inoffencif*
harvest (to)	*récolter*
Holy Grail	*Saint Graal*
lay people	*non spécialistes, profanes*
liver	*foie*
legacy	*héritage, legs*
lode	*filon, veine*
lung	*poumon*
offspring	*progéniture*
override (to)	*l'emporter sur*
menial tasks	*basses besognes*
mould (to)	*façonner*
MPs (Members of Parliament)	*députés*
patent (to)	*brevet, breveter*
patient	*malade*
pit against (to)	*opposer*
pool	*reservoir, bassin*
reach an agreement (to)	*parvenir à un accord*
recombinant DNA	*ADN recombinant*
rustlers	*voleurs*
scale	*échelle*
screening	*dépistage*
selective breeding	*élevage à base de sélection*
side-effects	*effets secondaires*
slumber	*reposer, sommeiller*
species	*espèce*
stringent	*rigoureux, strict*
surgery	*chirurgie*
tinker (to)	*manipuler, remanier*
tribe	*tribu*
weapons	*armes*

The arguments for and against genetic engineering

FOR

- It's the **'Holy Grail'** of biology
  - Full translation of the genetic message will enable medical researchers to identify the causes of thousands of unexplained physical and behavioural inherited disorders.

- **Gene therapy**
  - Scientists will be able to more accurately predict an individual's vulnerability to such obviously genetic diseases as cystic fibrosis and will eventually develop new drugs to treat or even prevent them.
  - The same is true for more common disorders like heart disease and cancer, which, at the very least, have large genetic **components**.

- **Germ-line therapy**, which would cause a patient to pass on the newly-introduced gene to his children, is attractive because it offers – thanks to the actual alteration of instructions in the human genome – the possibility of eradicating inherited conditions due to a **defective** gene.

- **People's well-being**
  - There are anxieties about genes that might change behaviour or physical features. But is it any different from cosmetic **surgery** or other attempts at self-improvement?
  - Immortal longings: the possibility of undoing **ageing**. People might be able to live much longer.

AGAINST

- The very thought of being able to **decipher** the entire human **genome**, and perhaps alter it, is alarming and will create many moral and ethical problems.
  - Genetic testing constitutes an invasion of privacy.
  - It **demeans** humans to have the very essence of their lives reduced to strings of letters in a computer data bank.

- **Genetic engineering** is tampering with nature and gene therapy, which causes changes in the patient's genetic make-up to be inherited by his descendants, should be banned.
  - **Gene therapy** will be used for improving a person's genetic **legacy** which is dangerous as there might be unforeseen and unwanted consequences. Mistakes might be made.

- The end result could very well be a *Brave New World*, very damaging to our human spirit.
  - Dangerous people or organisations might use **genetic engineering** to **mould** human beings to their liking. For example, they could breed a 'super race' or a race of slaves. Terrorists or mad dictators could exterminate ethnic groups. Fiction has given us the example of a gene of aggression being added to make test-tube babies fit for the army.
  - It could lead to more abortions and to discrimination against the 'genetically unfit'.
  - Employers could use the new genetics to screen their workforce.
  - Genetic **screening** could lead to genetic discrimination, where companies reject employees with defective genes and insurance companies rack up premiums for those predisposed to disease.

FINANCEMENT DES RETRAITES EN GRANDE-BRETAGNE

FINANCING RETIREMENT IN THE UNITED KINGDOM

FACTSHEET

Comme dans la plupart des pays développés, le nombre des personnes en âge de prendre leur retraite ou retraitées ne cesse de progresser en Grande Bretagne. Les 60/65 ans et plus représentent 20% de la population, ce qui alourdit la charge de l'État et explique en partie le changement de politique en matière de financement des retraites : le rôle de l'État diminue, les retraites d'entreprise et les plans de capitalisation se développent.

Le système de sécurité sociale repose sur une base d'*assurance obligatoire.* Tous les résidents versent des **cotisations**, originellement à **taux uniforme**, et reçoivent une **pension de base** – dès 65 ans pour les hommes, dès 60 ans pour les femmes –. A cette pension forfaitaire s'ajoutent des suppléments pour **personnes à charge**. Un nombre insuffisant de cotisations donne lieu à une minoration de la pension. La retraite est financée par les cotisations obligatoires des salariés et des employeurs, par celles des travailleurs indépendants et gérée par la caisse d'assurance vieillesse.

Par ailleurs, un système d'*assistance* offre aux personnes démunies de plus de 80 ans une pension minimale, sorte de fonds de solidarité vieillesse, versée **sous conditions de ressources** et de résidence. L'État peut verser un complément (**Income support**) lorsque la pension est en deçà du minimum vital. Ces types de pensions et **compléments de retraite** sont financés par l'impôt.

A la pension de base s'ajoute une **pension complémentaire**, fondée sur un système de cotisations et prestations **proportionnelles aux revenus**. Cette pension complémentaire proportionnelle est gérée soit par l'État, (**State Earnings Related Pension Scheme -SERPS-**), soit par l'un des 65. 000 régimes complémentaires.

Depuis la fin des années 80, le nombre des retraites complémentaires d'entreprise (**occupational pensions**) et des retraites individuelles (**Personal Equity Plans -PEPS-)** augmente. Les salariés sont incités à rompre le contrat qui les lie à l'État (**contracting out**), ce qui réduit leurs cotisations versées au **National Insurance Fund**, le but recherché étant le départ du SERPS vers le privé et la création d'emplois vacants. En outre, le calcul de la retraite complémentaire d'État (SERPS) est modifié, la pension de reversion des conjoints survivants réduite, pour permettre à l'État de substantielles économies.

Le financement des retraites d'entreprise provient des cotisations qu'employés et employeurs versent au fonds de pension de l'entreprise. La gestion de ces fonds de pension, qui prospèrent par investissements sur les marchés financiers, est assurée par l'employeur.

Les salariés peuvent choisir de se constituer une retraite individuelle, financée par un taux minimum de cotisations patronales et salariales, donnant lieu aux mêmes **déductions fiscales** que les retraites d'entreprises. Des banques, compagnies d'assurance ou sociétés immobilières gèrent ces cotisations.

Thinking the unthinkable

Health care and income in **retirement** are necessities with the awkward feature of also being, in economic terms, luxuries: as people grow richer, an ever-larger proportion of current income is devoted to them. Adding to this pressure, better health and advances in health care mean that the number of **elderly** people will grow – and the old are heavy consumers of state welfare in the form of pensions and health care.

The Economist

UK pension funds shift balance

There has been a significant shift in the portfolio balance of British pension funds which have a massive £18 billion to invest each year, a change of attitude that offers insights for private investors. (In 1996) the **pension funds** had 5.6% of their assets in cash, the highest level since 1990... In sharp contrast the pension industry's exposure to UK equities now stands at just 51.6%, its lowest level for a decade.

The European

Flat-rate pensions

Britain's post-war National Insurance system pays **flat-rate**, rather than the **earnings-related** benefits of France and Germany. During the sixties and seventies, Britain moved closer to the Continental pattern, introducing earnings-related supplements to pensions. After 1979, the reduction of the **basic pension** relative to earnings has taken Britain away from the European model.

The Guardian weekly

Under new ownership

If the organisation you work for changes hands, your first concern will be job security. Fortunately, in most cases you can be confident that the law will protect your rights under your employment contract.

What it may not protect, however, is your pension package, which will depend partly on your employer's corporate structure, partly on the method used to change ownership. Problems may arise when your employer sells the business as an asset. A high Court ruling confirms that TUPE* does not require the purchaser of a business to give transferring employees pension rights equivalent to those previously provided.

*TUPE: Transfer of Undertakings (Protection of Employment Regulations)

The Financial Times

Early retirement

Many of us have considered **early retirement** at some stage, but few can afford to give up work without careful planning. A 35-year-old man who plans to retire at 65 would need to contribute 12% of his salary each year to receive a retirement income equal to half his final salary.

If the same man chose to retire at 60, his **contributions** would have to go up to 17% to receive the same retirement income. If he wanted to quit at 55, he would have to invest almost a quarter of his salary into a **pension fund**.

The Sunday Times

EXTRA!!! CLASSI-FILES EXTRA!!!

THÈME

1. Au Royaume Uni, la pension de base complète est versée à tout retraité qui a cotisé pendant environ 9/10e de sa vie active. Par ailleurs, une retraite complémentaire d'état existe depuis 1959. Elle a été modifiée plusieurs fois.
2. Pour avoir droit à une pension de retraite, il faut avoir "l'âge de la retraite" – soit 65 ans pour un homme, 60 ans pour une femme – règlement qui constitue une forme de discrimination basée sur le sexe mais n'est pas contraire à la législation européenne.
3. Les cotisations aux caisses de retraite sont en général investies, par l'intermédiaire de sociétés d'assurances ou de banques, dans des valeurs boursières. Les fonds de pension doivent être gérés de façon à protéger les intérêts des cotisants.
4. Le principal souci de ceux qui sont contre les fonds de pension privés à base d'investissements financiers, c'est que ce procédé remet en cause l'aspect redistributif du système actuel.
5. Beaucoup de salariés qui ont travaillé dans cette société ont déclaré qu'ils n'auraient pas dû résilier leur plan de retraite d'état pour choisir une retraite professionnelle au sein de ce groupe.
6. Le Ministre de la Santé Publique nous accuse de ne pas avoir "pris nos précautions pour nos vieux jours". Il propose de diminuer les dépenses sociales et le montant des retraites, alors que les causes véritables sont d'ordre démographique et économique.
7. L'ennui avec les réformes de sécurité sociale et les réformes des systèmes de pensions en particulier, c'est qu'il peut se passer une quinzaine d'années avant qu'on puisse en voir les effets.

EXTRA!!! CLASSI-FILES EXTRA!!!

VERSION

1. Greater longevity and fewer births mean that people of working age are a diminishing fraction of the population. As a result, taxpayers will eventually be unable to finance **benefits**, even at current levels.
2. The projections for 2020 show that state spendings on pensions are around 12% of GDP in France, 14% in Germany, with further rises to come. In the United Kingdom, they are around 5 per cent, and falling.
3. Last year, the Prime Minister asserted that the state pension would remain the foundation for security in **retirement** and he repeated his pledge to protect all those in genuine need.
4. Employees are allowed to invest 15% of their salary a year into an **occupational scheme**. The limits for holders of personal pension plans are scaled according to age.
5. The **Inland Revenue** places limits on the amount of money we can put into **pension funds** to prevent abuse of the **tax relief** on pension **contributions**.
6 50 years ago, less than half those **eligible** reached the official retirement age. Today, eight out of ten attain the lower retirement age of 60, which might partly explain the increase in public spending on **the elderly.**
7. In the American social security pension programme, the social security trust fund has held the present surplus of **payroll-tax** receipts over the benefits in the form of government bonds.

1. In the United Kingdom, a full basic pension is granted to any pensioner who paid contributions during about 9/10th of his working life. Besides, an additional state pension was created in 1959. It has been modified several times.
2. To get a retirement pension, you must have reached 'pensionable age' – i.e. 65 for a man, 60 for a woman – a rule which discriminates on grounds of sex but is not contrary to EC law.
3. Contributions to pension funds are generally invested in securities, through insurance companies or banks. Pension funds must be managed so as to protect the interests of the contributors.
4. The major concern of those who oppose individual investment-based pension funds is that this scheme undermines the redistributive aspect of the present system.
5. Many wage-earners who worked in this company declared that they should not have opted out of the state additional pension plan to set up an occupational pension scheme within this group.
6. The Health Secretary accuses us of 'not having made proper provision for our old age'. He wants to cut welfare spending and pensions while the actual causes are demographic and economic.
7. The trouble with social security reforms, and with pension schemes reforms in particular, is that it could be some fifteen years from now before the results can be seen.

1. Une plus grande longévité et un nombre décroissant de naissances signifient que la population active constitue une fraction réduite de la population. Par conséquent, les contribuables finiront par ne plus pouvoir financer les prestations, même à leur niveau actuel.
2. Les prévisions pour 2020 concernant les dépenses de l'État en matière de retraites, atteignent environ 12% du Produit Intérieur Brut en France, 14% en Allemagne, avec une tendance à la hausse. Au Royaume Uni, elles représentent environ 5% du PIB, avec une tendance à la baisse.
3. L'an passé, le Premier Ministre a affirmé que la pension d'état continuerait à assurer la sécurité de base de la retraite et il a répété qu'il s'engageait à protéger les personnes réellement dans le besoin.
4. Les employés ont le droit d'investir 15% de leur salaire annuel dans un plan de retraite professionnelle. Les plafonds imposés aux titulaires de ces plans de retraite individuelle varient en fonction de l'âge.
5. Le fisc plafonne les sommes d'argent que nous pouvons verser à des caisses de retraite individuelle pour éviter des déductions fiscales abusives sur les cotisations sociales.
6. Il y a 50 ans, moins de la moitié de ceux qui pouvaient prétendre à la retraite atteignaient l'âge officiel. Aujourd'hui, 8 personnes sur 10 atteignent 60 ans, âge minimum requis pour la retraite, ce qui pourrait en partie expliquer l'accroissement des dépenses publiques pour personnes âgées.
7. Dans le programme américain de retraites d'État, la caisse de sécurité sociale conserve l'excédent actuel des charges patronales par rapport aux pensions versées sous forme de bons du Trésor.

VOCABULARY

additional (earnings-related) pension	*retraite complémentaire (soumise à cotisation)*
basic pension	*pension de base (forfaitaire)*
benefits	*prestations, allocations*
claim for retirement	*demande de pension (to make a claim for)*
claimant	*demandeur (to claim: déposer une demande), récipiendaire, bénéficiaire*
company superannuation scheme	*retraite professionnelle, d'entreprise*
contracting-out	*quitter le plan de retraite d'état pour une retraite d'entreprise*
contribution	*cotisation (de sécurité sociale)*
demographic pattern	*configuration démographique*
dependant	*personne à charge (*adult dependant, child dependant)
early retirement	*pré-retraite*
earnings-related	*proportionnel aux gains/revenus*
elderly, adj	*vieux, âgé (the elderly: les personnes âgées)*
entitlement	*qualification (to be entitled to a pension: avoir droit à une pension)*
flat-rate	*à taux uniforme*
graduated retirement benefit	*retraite proportionnelle (en fractionnements progressifs)*
income support	*fonds d'aide au maintien du revenu, complément de ressources*
inland payments	*contributions directes*
Inland revenue	*Fisc*
means-tested, adj.	*sous condition de ressources*
National Insurance Fund	*Caisse Nationale d'Assurance Vieillesse*
occupational pension scheme	*plan de retraite d'entreprise, retraite professionnelle*
payroll tax	*charges sociales, cotisations patronales*
pension fund	*fonds de pension, caisse de retraite individuelle*
pensionable age	*âge légal de la retraite*
pensioner premium	*complément-retraite sous condition de ressources sans cotisation préalable*
Personal Equity Plans	*plans de retraite personnelle*
Personal Pension Schemes (PEPS)	*régimes de retraite personnelle*
personal pension	*plan de retraite privée, personnelle*
reduced pension	*pension réduite, minorée*
retirement pension	*pension de base (étatique)*
SERPS (State Earnings Related Pension Scheme)	*régime de retraite complémentaire d'État*
superannuation scheme	*plan de pension d'entreprise*
tax rebate, tax relief	*déduction fiscale, exonération*
to be disqualified	*perdre ses droits*
to be eligible (for a pension)	*avoir droit (à la retraite), ayant-droit*
to defer (entitlement, pension)	*repousser le moment (de recevoir une prestation, la retraite)*
to opt out	*choisir de ne pas participer*

■ Demography

Population of the United Kingdom (thousands)

Analyse the above table and comment on the growth of **the elderly** population. What does this increase imply for the working population?

	1901	1931	1961	1981	1991	1995	1997	2001**
all ages	38237	46038	52807	56352	57806	58606	59009	59618
65-74	1278	2461	3977	5195	5067	5127	5006	4963
75-84	470	844	1885	2675	3136	3054	3243	3296
over 85	61	113	346	602	896	1044	1088	1163
pensionable age*	2387	4421	7747	10031	10597	10652	10691	10757

*Pensionable age = men over 65, women over 60 ; **projected. Source: Annual Abstract of Statistics 1999

The growth of the elderly population is not evenly distributed: the number of very old people has been increasing faster than the number of people aged 65-74. Which elements could explain this phenomenon ? What are the consequences of such a **demographic pattern** for the Welfare state, in terms of costs?

■ Older, dearer

The table shows that

- In some countries women retire earlier than men, yet, they often live longer, which implies that they will cost more to the state. The current trend is towards similar retirement ages for both sexes. Give your opinion.
- Some countries spend more than others on public pensions. Some may spend little on pensions because of economic difficulties, some don't spend much because the government policy is "to roll back the frontiers of the state" and to encourage private schemes. Discuss the case of Great Britain.

	Public pension as % of GDP[5]	Retirement age male	female
Britain[1]	5,9	65	60
France[2]	9,7	60	60
Germany[3]	8,2	65	65
Italy[4]	10,9	62	57
Netherlands	7,5	65	65
Spain	6,8	65	65
Sweden	9,5	65	65

1. retirement for women to be raised to 65 by 2020. 2. subject to 38 years'contributions (40 years from 2002). 3. Retirement at 63 allowed if 35 years'insurance paid. 4. Retirement to be gradually equalised to 65. 5. 1993. Source: Eurolink Age, OECD.

■ Public *vs* private retirement pension schemes

After the death of R. Maxwell, the press tycoon, people found out that the pension funds entrusted to his group had been dilapidated: pensioners were robbed their working life savings. It might be safer to pay **contributions** to the state, in order to get a full pension rather than to entrust one's savings to a private enterprise.

■ Early retirement *vs* a prolonged working life

No European country enjoys full employment and, even in the UK, unemployment figures are high. **Early retirement** could be a good means to create vacancies, yet, figures show that more and more people go on working after retirement age.

■ Flat-rate *vs* income-related contributions

Flat-rate contributions are said to be a means to redistribute wealth, to create a safety net and protect the elderly against poverty, while they are free to constitute some additional pension scheme as they see fit.

Income-related contributions induce people to contribute during their working life in order to safeguard their living standards in old age.

LES MINORITÉS SEXUELLES

SEXUAL MINORITIES

FACTSHEET

Le 24 avril 1997, le Président Clinton s'adresse au Congrès pour l'encourager à approuver une loi portant sur la fin de la discrimination liée à l'orientation sexuelle dans le domaine de l'emploi, l'ENDA (Employment Non-Discrimination Act). Bill Clinton rappelle que la diversité n'est pas une faiblesse. Pourtant quarante et un états pratiquent cette discrimination aux USA. La carte ci-dessous présente les états régis par les "**Sodomy Laws**', lois qui condamnent une sexualité différente et qui, par réduction, sont utilisées à l'encontre de l'homosexualité.

Comment interpréter cette carte ? Curieusement, celle-ci ne reflète pas les grands courants religieux auxquels on pourrait s'attendre. Les états du nord, pourtant très puritains et très respectueux du code social, ont abandonné les lois favorisant la discrimination envers les minorités. En revanche, les états du sud sont plus conservateurs. Dans les états qui apparaissent sous des rayures grisées, des lois extrêmement strictes régissent les relations dans le couple marié et a fortiori celles en dehors du mariage.

Une constante, d'ordre économique, semble se dégager, celle du développement industriel. Les états fortement industrialisés ont adopté des lois nouvelles, tels ceux de la côte ouest avec la haute technologie, la côte est et le Nord avec ses mégapoles (Chicago, Philadelphie, New York).

Toutefois, le démocrate Clinton fait une exception pour l'armée, 'the military' dans chacun des textes qu'il propose. Tout au plus, concède-t-il le célèbre 'Don't ask, don't tell', un compromis en faveur des militaires qu'il contrebalance aussitôt par une loi sur la protection du mariage 'Defense of Marriage Act'.

Par ailleurs, le parti démocrate n'est plus le seul à défendre le droit des minorités sexuelles. Ainsi, les voix inattendues de soixante-trois membres du parti républicain ont empêché l'abrogation du texte de loi protégeant les employés fédéraux homosexuels.

En Grande-Bretagne, des membres du gouvernement de Tony Blair ainsi que des ministres des gouvernements précédents ont été exposés à des dénonciations publiques dans des tabloïds tels que *The Sun* (quotidien populaire ou "organe de presse de caniveau", selon ses détracteurs). Cependant, tous n'ont pas démissionné, ce qui dénote un changement d'attitude.

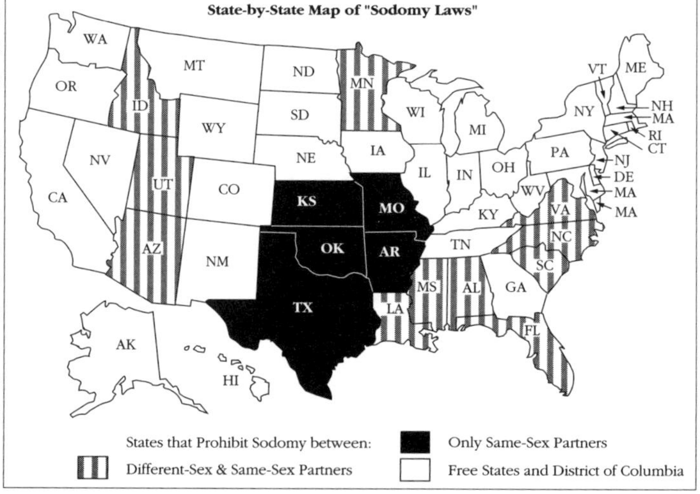

State-by-State Map of "Sodomy Laws"

Europe's Gay Politics

European governments are tampering liberalism with tradition as they legislate for gay rights. The ages of sexual consent (below) vary, as does current policy.

France, 15 years old: Last week the National Assembly stalled on a bill giving gay couples **benefits** that married couples enjoy.

Germany, 16: Schröder campaigned for an antidiscrimination law and a 'registered partnership' right for homosexuals.

Ireland, 17: Since homosexuality was decriminalized in 1993, gays can join the Army and get other equal-treatment **benefits**.

Italy, 14: In July the city commissions of Pisa and Florence voted to view gay partnerships like **common-law marriages.**

U.K., 16-18: The House of Lords voted in July not to make gay sex legal at 16 – a bill the House of Commons had approved.

Newsweek

Supports Gay Bakersfield Teacher

Ruling : school district violated state law by removing students from his classroom

Los Angeles, March 9, 1999. ...The Commissioner ruled that Rio Bravo-Greeley Union School District official's **yanking** 15 students from the classroom of award-winning teacher James D. Merrick, Ph.D. was a violation of state law. The California labor code prohibits employment discrimination based on actual or perceived **sexual orientation**.

Press Releases, Internet

Public attitudes are changing

Rupert Murdoch's *Sun*, London most over-the-top **antigay tab**, vowed not to out people in its pages, except in cases of 'overwhelming public interest.' 'We recognize,' said the editorial, 'that public attitudes are changing.'

...Most of the change is legislative; many of the Continent's left-of-center governments are debating **gay-friendly** policies or thinking about it. The European Parliament in Strasbourg has passed **a raft of resolutions** demanding equal treatment for gays and lesbians in EU countries. As established political parties have begun to address gay **issues**, gay **activists** have changed their methods.

Newsweek

Mainstream

In movies, gays were first ignored, then scorned. By the early '90s, with AIDS doing its dirty work, gays got to be pitied. But they were typically portrayed as a separate species, the exotic *other*... Gays have **come out of the celluloid closet** and into **the** movie **mainstream**.

Mainstream milestones in films on homosexuals : *Philadelphia*, 1993 (Tom Hanks as a gay man dying of AIDS. $77,3 mil.), *The Birdcage*, 1996 (Robin Williams and Nathan Lane hit a joyful new style in family values. $124 mil.) and *In & Out*, 1997 (Kevin Kline isn't gay - is he? Just ask Tom Selleck. $64 mil.).

TimeState Labor Commissioner

EXTRA!!! CLASSI-FILES EXTRA!!!

THÈME

1. (Grande-Bretagne) La Chambre des Communes s'est prononcée, lundi 25 janvier 1999, en faveur de l'abaissement, de 18 à 16 ans, de l'âge de la majorité sexuelle pour les homosexuels. Ce vote en seconde lecture a été acquis par 313 voix contre 130, ce qui reflète à peu près la majorité travailliste, favorable à la loi, contre l'opposition des Conservateurs. Le texte doit maintenant être renvoyé à la Chambre des Lords, laquelle, en juillet 1998, avait repoussé ce même projet du gouvernement Blair de dépénalisation des relations homosexuelles à partir de 16 ans. (AFP.)
2. (A propos de ce sénateur, B. Delanoë qui, sur la chaîne de télévision M6, dévoile son homosexualité) ...Il ne livre de lui-même que ce qu'il a décidé de livrer. Mais n'est-il pas en train, sous nos yeux, de faire voler en éclats la fameuse "exception française", celle du respect par la presse de la vie privée des hommes publics ? Ce qui nous séparait encore des Américains et des Britanniques, cette mystérieuse barrière qui interdirait, en France, à un journal d'oser comme en Grande-Bretagne de demander à la "une" : "Sommes-nous gouvernés par une mafia gay ?", et rend jusqu'à présent inimaginable une affaire Lewinsky... ?
3. En pleine ascension, Amélie Mauresmo a révélé son homosexualité, ce qui ne plaît guère aux responsables du circuit, mais ne semble pas déranger ses sponsors. ... Dans le tennis féminin à son apogée, le politiquement incorrect, qui, pour les mêmes causes, avait eu raison de certains des sponsors de Martina Navratilova, est en passe de devenir un bel argument de vente.

EXTRA!!! CLASSI-FILES EXTRA!!!

VERSION

1. What she (Ellen DeGeneres) hasn't been able to bring herself to do, until now, is use the word **gay** along with 'I am' in public. Indeed, for a lot of men and women whose livelihood depends on the goodwill of millions, those may be the scariest words in the English language.
2. Clinton cannily used the saintly Rosa Parks to ask for passage of the Employment Nondiscrimination Act and the Hate Crimes Prevention Act, but he didn't say what they were: laws to advance gay equality... After last year's killing of Matthew Shephard* , the **hate-crimes bill** actually has a chance.
   * The twenty-year-old Matthew Shepard, who was gay, was murdered and his body was stretched along a Wyoming fence. His murder is perceived as a lynching because he was killed to make a point.
3. (G.B.) Last month a Labour Party minister – married, with a daughter – **resigned** after being robbed near one of London's best-known gay-cruising zones. The ritual of political humiliation quickly followed. The **tabloids** did daily battle in three-inch **headlines**. There was a **resignation** letter to Prime Minister Tony Blair, a red-eyed press conference, a career in ruins.
4. ... Two days after his announcement, Agriculture Minister Nick Brown was stomping around in gumboots, visiting Devon farmers, who told him they didn't mind if he was gay as long as he did something about the sorry state of British agriculture. Peter Mandelson, the Trade and Industry secretary, refused to discuss his sexuality – and the papers let him be.

1. (Great Britain) On Monday 25 January 1999, the House of Commons voted in favour of lowering the age of sexual majority for homosexuals from 18 to 16. This second reading was adopted by 313 yes-votes against 130, which, by and large, reflects the Labour party's majority over the Conservatives, the latter being opposed to the bill. It must now be sent back to the House of Lords which, in July 1998, rebuffed the same plan by the Blair government to decriminalise homosexual sex from the age of 16. (AFP)
2. (Concerning B. Delanöe, the senator who **came out** on the M6 television channel) … He only discloses what he wants to disclose about himself. And isn't he breaching the famous 'French exception', by which the media respects the private lives of public figures? This is what differentiated us from Americans and Brits, this mysterious barrier which prevented a French newspaper from asking the type of questions that are splashed **on the** British **front pages**, such as 'Are we governed by a gay Mafia?' and made a Monicagate unimaginable in France.
3. Amélie Mauresmo, a rising star on the tennis circuit, has **come out of the closet.** This hardly meets with the agreement of the tennis world but does not seem to bother her sponsors. … What was politically incorrect when feminine tennis was at its height and led Martine Navratilova's sponsors to withdraw now seems to be becoming a very effective selling point.

1. Ce qu'elle (Ellen DeGeneres) n'a pas encore pu se résoudre à faire jusqu'à maintenant, est de prononcer à la suite et en public les mots "homosexuelle" et "Je suis". Car pour un grand nombre d'hommes et de femmes dont les moyens d'existence dépendent du bon vouloir d'une multitude , ces mots là sont les plus risqués de la langue.
2. Clinton a très habilement utilisé l'inattaquable Rosa Parks pour solliciter le passage des textes de loi sur l'ENDA (la non discrimination en matière d'emploi) et sur la prévention des délits d'incitation à la haine, sans dire qu'il s'agissait de lois promouvant l'égalité des homosexuels… Suite à l'assassinat de Matthew Shephard* l'an dernier, la loi sur l'incitation à la haine a, de fait, toutes les chances d'être votée.
   * : Matthew Shephard un homosexuel de vingt et un ans, a été assassiné et son corps exposé sur une barrière dans l'état du Wyoming. Ce meurtre est assimilé à un lynchage car il a été exécuté pour servir d'exemple.
3. (Grande-Bretagne) Le mois dernier, un ministre du Parti travailliste – marié, une fille – a démissionné après avoir été dévalisé près d'un des coins chauds de Londres réputés gays. Le rituel de l'humiliation politique a tout de suite suivi. La presse populaire est passée à une offensive quotidienne en manchettes hautes de sept centimètres. Conséquence : une lettre de démission adressée au Premier Ministre Tony Blair, une conférence de presse les yeux rougis et une carrière en ruine.
4. Deux jours après sa révélation, le Secrétaire d'État à l'Agriculture, Nick Brown, chaussé de bottes de caoutchouc, venait d'un pas lourd à la rencontre des agriculteurs du comté du Devon, qui lui dirent que cela leur était égal qu'il fût gay du moment qu'il s'engageait à remédier à la situation déplorable de l'agriculture britannique. Peter Mandelson, Ministre du Commerce, a refusé de discuter de sa sexualité et les journaux l'ont laissé tranquille.

VOCABULARY

Nouns

abortion .... *avortement*
an activist .... *un militant*
addiction .... *la dépendance*
AIDS .... *sida*
an awareness .... *conscience, sensibilisation*
(Domestic Partner) benefits .... *allocations (versées au conjoint)*
bias .... *parti pris ; discrimination*
bigotry .... *tendance doctrinaire*
a bill .... *projet de loi*
civil rights .... *les droits civiques*
common law marriage *concubinage*
a controversy .... *une controverse*
fairness .... *impartialité, équité*
the gutter press .... *la presse de 'caniveau', à sensation*
hate-crime bill / legislation .... *loi interdisant l'incitation à la haine*
health care .... *la Santé (prise en charge des soins)*
homophobia .... *phobie des homosexuels*
illness .... *maladie*
an issue .... *un problème, une question*
mainstream .... *le courant dominant, la norme*
outing ; to out .... *fait de révéler l'homosexualité d'une personne contre son gré*
resignation ; to resign .. *démission ; démissionner*
sexual orientation .... *penchants sexuels*
a sin ; to sin .... *un péché ; commettre un péché*
Sodomy Laws .... *lois américaines qui régissent la sexualité*
a tabloid / a tab .... *un tabloïd, un journal populaire*
trial ; to try .... *procès, jugement ; juger*
Middle America .... *Américains aisés aux idées conservatrices*
a raft of resolutions .... *une série de mesures*

Phrases

to come out of the closet .... *"sortir du placard" c'est-à-dire révéler son homosexualité*
to be at risk .... *mettre en danger*
to be in the headlines / on the front page *faire la une (des journaux), défrayer la chronique*

Adjectives

adrift .... *à la dérive*
alternative (lifestyle) .... *(mode de vie) non-conventionnel*
anti-gay .... *contre les homosexuels*
controversial .... *controversé ; discutable*
gay-friendly .... *favorable aux homosexuels*
HIV-positive .... *séropositif*
homophobic .... *homophobe*
lethal .... *mortel*
mainstream .... *traditionnel, classique, (par opposition à "marginal")*
nationwide .... *sur l'ensemble du territoire, à l'échelle nationale*
straight .... *hétérosexuel*
supportive .... *encourageant, réconfortant*
unfair .... *injuste*

Verbs

to acknowledge .... *reconnaître, admettre*
to back .... *apporter son soutien*
to ban .... *interdire*
to blame sb for sthg .... *reprocher quelque chose à quelqu'un*
to debunk .... *dénoncer*
to demonstrate .... *manifester*
to fire sb .... *renvoyer, licencier*
to implement .... *mettre en application, exécuter*
to jeopardise .... *mettre en danger*
to legitimize .... *légaliser*
to march .... *défiler*
to nurture .... *nourrir, contribuer au développement*
to play off .... *se faire concurrence*
to prosecute .... *poursuivre en justice*
to rule .... *statuer*
to sue .... *intenter un procès*
to turn somebody away *rejeter quelqu'un*
to urge .... *exhorter,*
to yank .... (ici) *renvoyer*

'TV is one of our culture's greatest teachers, but just how and what does prime time teach? Any careful observer of human nature knows that what we immerse ourselves in, we become. A culture that immerses itself in casual, illicit sex will become a culture **adrift** in a sea of moral irresponsibility. Parents should stay on the alert - the flooding is still building!' (Randall MURPHREE, editor, *American Family Association Journal*, quoted in *Time*, April 14, 1997)

Does television influence society or reflect it? Does Ellen Morgan's coming out in what is still our massest medium legitimize homosexuality, or does the sponsorship of a bottom-line business like ABC merely reflect its acceptance by a significant portion of the population?
The answer is both. TV and culture **play off** each other in ways that are hard to codify. You cannot reduce these complex reverberations to a black-or-white issue. ◆ It would be a mistake, however, to think of TV history as one long, uninterrupted drift toward license. Moral values are, of course, relative. ...Today there are new taboos. Nobody's going to do an **abortion** on a sitcom today. (*Time*)

Can politics cause hate?
Gay **activists** linked recent conservative pronouncements on homosexuality (like ads saying gays can be 'cured') to the Shepard murder, saying that such talk **nurtures bigotry**. They **urged** Congress and the states to pass **hate-crimes** legislation to stiffen penalties for crimes motivated by **bias** against gender, race, **sexual orientation** or disability. (*Time*) ◆ 'You should try to show them a way to deal with [homosexuality] just like alcohol... or sex **addiction** ... or kleptomaniacs. (The Senate majority leader on TV in June 1998, in *Time)*

What about religion?
'the acceptance of homosexuality is the last step in the decline of Gentile civilization.' (Pat Robertson, of the Christian Broadcasting Network-. Robertson warned that hurricanes could hit Orlando, Fla., because of gay events there. ◆ In January [1998] a 39-year-old Sicilian, Alfredo Ormando, burned himself to death in St Peter's Square to protest the Vatican's **anti-gay** policies. ◆ The Catholic church reminded that it didn't condemn homosexuality itself but only any sexual act outside marriage. (The Lutheran church in Germany celebrates ceremonies for homosexuals, see *Newsweek*.)

What about jokes made about people who are not 'straight'? Isn't that some form of social conditioning?
In the film *Philadelphia* : at the racket club, Andrew Beckett, the lawyer suffering from AIDS, hears one of the managing partners crack a joke about gays and explains at the **trial** that at the time he felt 'relieved' that he had never told his employer about his homosexuality. ➪These jokes reveal a lot about our mentalities. Minorities of any kind often fall prey to jesters. From these jokes we may feel conditioned to react in a certain way as to what is manly and what isn't.

Two different attitudes

- Homosexuality, like sexual addiction, alcoholism or kleptomania, can be cured.
- People should have compassion toward individuals that have *problems*, i.e. that are homosexuals.
- The Catholic Church does not condemn homosexuality itself but only any sexual act outside marriage.
- It is a **sin**. The Bible is very clear on this.
- Some politicians debunk the 'false god of gay rights'.
- Gay activists are going too far when they decide to **out** a public figure. **Outing** is an extremist attitude which should be condemned.
- what about the traditional family model if homosexuality becomes a matter of fact? Society is **at risk!**/is being **jeopardised**!

- Homosexuality is not a mental **illness**.
- An **alternative lifestyle**, a different **sexual orientation**, should not be regarded as a *problem*.
- Acceptance of a difference, tolerance are needed. In fact, homosexuals are claiming a right to 'indifference', the right to go by unnoticed.
- It's not a moral imperative to be a heterosexual.
- Gays are citizens that have rights.
- **Bigots** are more to be feared than gays **coming out**. They are demonizing gays and encouraging violence such as the Shephard murder. They think their opinion is the only correct one. Bigotry is dangerous and so is religious conditioning.
- 50% of marriages end up in a divorce!

TONY BLAIR AND THE PROBLEMS OF THE BRITISH EDUCATION SYSTEM

LES RÉFORMES DU SYSTÈME ÉDUCATIF EFFECTUÉES PAR TONY BLAIR

FACTSHEET

Tony Blair was returned to office in May 1997, 50 years after the 1947 Education Act, prolonging the war effort, proposed to give all British children fairer chances at school and move Britain towards a more egalitarian society. The Act gave the Department of Education the power to control local education authorities in charge of primary, secondary and further education in their areas. The 1947 Education Act provided for a test at the age of 11 (11+) which inaugurated a tripartite system of secondary education. It has been estimated that after 11+, 20% of children considered to be academically minded went to grammar schools leading to universities, the most prestigious of them remaining Oxford and Cambridge. Secondary modern schools offered a less rigorous curriculum to 75% of children, while 5% of technically minded children went to technical schools.

However, the tripartite system came under increasing criticisms in the 50s and 60s. People belonging to the left wing political parties but also some Conservatives considered the 11+ test unfair and divisive. Voices were heard louder and louder, **urging** the replacement of the tripartite system by a comprehensive school capable of giving their chances to children of all **backgrounds** and abilities. The comprehensive school movement was **given a boost** by the Labour Party victory at the 1964 election. Harold Wilson's government encouraged local authorities to go comprehensive, **all but** a few obliged.

Along with comprehensive schools came a wind of change in education **heralded by** the Plowden Report in 1967. Teaching in primary schools became child centred. Desks were **bunched together**, teachers spent less time talking, paid less attention to the curriculum and encouraged pupils to work at their own **pace,** on projects they had chosen.

Having to cater for pupils of all ethnic origins and conditions the comprehensive schools were admittedly facing difficult situations. A balanced **assessment** of their **achievements** is difficult to make. **There is no denying that** a lot of them **coped gallantly** with their problems. It is also true that some of the reforms introduced brought some **unwanted effects**. Disruption of discipline, falling **standards** in the learning of the three R's, reading, writing, and reckoning were noted in some schools. Throughout the Thatcher and Major years there was a tension between a Conservative govern-ment and left wing Labour education authorities. The Thatcher government gave schools the possibility to opt out of the Local Authority system and place themselves under the direct control of the Department of Education. That's the context in which both labour's election manifesto and the on-going debate about education in the British media have to be read. The proclaimed aims of the government are: zero tolerance for underperformance, quality education guaranteed for all four-year-olds, a new **focus put** on standards in primary schools, attacking educational disadvantage, realising the potential of new technologies, the cost of student maintenance to be repaid by graduates on an **income-related basis**.

Innovative strategies are needed where, as happens now, over 30% of 14-and 15-years old regularly **play truant** from school and where fewer than 25% of 11-year-olds reach the nationally determined attainment norm in Maths English and Science New Times .
The Chief Inspector of Schools, Chris Wooddhead, at a London lecture, said it was time to end the **complacency** that had damaged the profession. Head teachers especially should take responsibility for **'blowing the whistle'** on staff who were not up to scratch; and those forced to leave the profession in that way should not be rewarded with huge **redundancy payments**.

The Guardian

Doug McAvoy, general secretary of the National Union of Teachers said 'Teachers know that linking their pay to pupil achievement and annual appraisals of their performances will divide schools... will not benefit children's education nor raise the status and morale of teachers'.

The Independent

The four-year target is to connect every school to the internet. The idea is to allow pupils access to remote libraries and museums, enable teachers to share their ideas and parents to help their children with their homework (BBC Coverage of the Labour Party Conference)
However. 'The government has promised not to be dogmatic about the teaching methods it pushes, but to live by the maxim that 'what counts is what **works**'.

The Economist

Labour is now intervening in schools far more actively than any previous government, Labour or Tory... Mr Blunkett says...'I believe in discipline, solid mental arithmetic, learning to read and write accurately, plenty of homework, increasing expectations'.

The Economist

The government is to seize control of one of Britain's worst education authorities after the inspectors found it was still **failing** pupils. Ministers are set to take the unprecedented step of staging a direct take-over of Hackney council's education department and... to invite private firms and neighbouring councils to **bid for** the troubled management of the troubled north-east London authority.

The Independent

Good teaching deserves decent rewards. For many, however, pay remains stuck at around £ 22,500 after seven years in the classroom, with the only prospect of earning more by taking on extra management responsibilities. That is why the teachers **green paper outlines** plans for good teachers to get an **uplift** in pay of up to 10 per cent for strong performances.

The Guardian

The 'progressive' revolution in Britain's schools is being reversed. Though progressivism had become the orthodoxy by the mid-1970s, things did not turn out the way the Plowden committee had intended... The schools adopted an extremely **informal** style in which pupils could do what they liked. Chaos ensued with the newspapers full of **lurid** stories about it...

The Economist

THÈME

1. Tout le monde doit se sentir concerné si nous voulons que nos enfants soient convenablement éduqués.
2. Le livre vert contient une série de propositions novatrices qui offrent des possibilités de formation continue aux professeurs. S'ils sont prêts à relever les défis de l'an 2000, ils n'ont pas de souci à se faire, ils seront évalués équitablement et justement récompensés. Monsieur Blunkett veut que le gouvernement dépense trois milliards de plus pour l'éducation au cours des trois prochaines années.
3. Nous sommes tous fascinés par les savants et le pouvoir qu'ils exercent dans notre monde. Les livres de science-fiction se vendent bien, et pourtant peu de filles choisissent d'étudier les sciences à l'école.
4. Nous n'avons pas intérêt à sermonner les adultes, mais la société a un rôle à jouer dans l'éducation des enfants, nous voulons seulement aider les parents à faire tout ce qu'ils peuvent…
5. Les dernières inspections montrent que certaines écoles ont des résultats bien au-dessous du niveau national… Elles prétendent que les choses s'améliorent. Les inspecteurs pensent que les progrès sont beaucoup trop lents. Ils veulent que les autorités locales agissent d'urgence sinon le gouvernement prendra en charge les écoles défaillantes.
6. Le psychologue suisse Jean Piaget a étudié systématiquement la façon dont les enfants apprennent. Il pense qu'ils se développent mentalement en passant par quatre étapes importantes.

VERSION

1. Young people from some districts of Aberdeen are to be given a chance to take up hobbies or interests they might not otherwise be able to pursue. By avoiding boredom, raising self-esteem and developing personal skills, the organisers aim to reduce the likelihood of youngsters being drawn into negative pastimes like drugs.
2. Disruptive children are to be the subject of a £500m drive to tackle truancy and reduce the number of exclusions from schools. 'Bunking off' lessons will no longer be an option. Instead of being banned from schools, children who disrupt classes will be put into special units supervised by teachers specially trained to cope with unruly children. *The Guardian*
3. The British have an almost unshakeable belief in the existence of that mystical governing elite, the Establishment. A network of exclusive London clubs supposedly play host to a cluster of civil servants, business men and financiers who are united by family, education and conservative views and who allegedly run the country. *The Guardian*
4. The government are determined to break down barriers between old and young in order to encourage respect for the elderly. The government is also going to urge school to invite grandparents to become voluntary classroom assistants and involve them in helping children with homework. *The Observer*

1. Everyone needs to feel concerned if we want our children to be properly educated.
2. **The Green Paper** contains a series of innovative proposals providing for in-service training for teachers. If they are ready to meet the challenges of the year 2000 they have nothing to worry about, they will be assessed fairly and properly rewarded. Mr Blunkette wants the government to spend an extra £3bn for education over the next three years.
3. We are all fascinated by scientists and the power they **wield** in our world, but few girls choose to study science at school.
4. We have no interest in preaching to adults, but society does have a role in bringing up kids, we only want parents to do their utmost.
5. The last inspections show that the results of some schools are well below national standards. They claim that things are improving. Inspectors think that they progress much too slowly. They want local authorities to act urgently otherwise they will take over failing schools.
6. The Swiss psychologist Jean Piaget has studied systematically how children learn. He thinks they grow mentally by going through four important stages.

1. Les jeunes gens de certains districts d'Aberdeen vont pouvoir pratiquer certaines activités de loisir auxquelles ils n'auraient pas normalement eu accès. En leur évitant l'ennui, en leur apprenant à prendre confiance en eux et à développer des compétences personnelles les organisateurs du projet espèrent les détourner de passe-temps négatifs comme la drogue.
2. Les enfants difficiles vont faire l'objet d'un investissement de 500 millions de livre sterling qui seront dépensées pour lutter contre l'école buissonnière et limiter le nombre d'exclusions des écoles. "Sécher" les cours ne sera plus de mise. Au lieu d'être mis à la porte, les enfants qui perturbent les cours seront remis à des unités spéciales entre les mains de professeurs spécialement formés pour s'occuper d'enfants indisciplinés.
3. Les Britanniques ont une croyance quasi immuable en l'existence de cette élite gouvernementale mythique, l'*Establishment.* Tout un réseau de clubs londoniens très fermés sont censés héberger une théorie de hauts fonctionnaires, d'hommes d'affaires et de financiers, qui sont unis par des liens familiaux, et l'éducation qu'ils ont reçue, partagent les mêmes idées conservatrices, et dit-on, gouvernent le pays.
4. Le gouvernement est résolu à briser les barrières qui séparent les vieux des jeunes afin d'encourager le respect des anciens. Le gouvernement va aussi exhorter les écoles à inviter les grands-parents à devenir auxiliaire d'enseignement volontaire dans les classes et à aider les enfants à faire leurs devoirs.

VOCABULARY

achievement	*réalisation, ce qui a été accompli*
all but a few	*presque tous (toutes)*
assessment	*évaluation*
background	*origines sociales*
bid for (to)	*essayer d'obtenir quelque chose*
blowing the whistle	*tirer la sonnette d'alarme*
bunched	*mis en ronds*
chalk and talk	*la craie et la parole*
complacency	*complaisance*
coped gallantly	*ont fait face courageusement*
denying (there is no)	*on ne saurait nier que*
deprived background	*milieu défavorisé*
devise	*imaginer concevoir*
failing	*défaillant(e)*
fluency	*aisance d'expression*
focus	*point focal, sur lequel on consacre son attention*
give a boost (to)	*donner un coup de pouce à*
Green Paper	*document qui contient des idées obtenues au cours d'une consultation préalable à l'élaboration d'une loi*
heralded by	*annoncé par*
huge redundancy payment	*de grosses indemnités de paiement*
income related basis	*proportionné au revenu*
informal	*détendu et bon enfant*
lurid	*décrit en recherchant le sensationnel*
outline	*les grandes lignes*
pace	*rythme*
preposterous	*ridicule*
rewarded	*récompensé*
rote learning	*apprendre mécaniquement*
trade	*métier*
trendy	*à la mode*
truant (to play)	*faire l'école buissonnière*
undemanding	*pas assez exigeant*
unwanted effects	*effets pervers*
up to scratch	*à la hauteur*
uplift (to)	*rehausser*
urge (to)	*exhorter à*
wield (to)	*exercer un pouvoir*
work (to)	*marcher*

Progressive education

Casting your mind back to your own school days and considering how you would like to educate your own children examine the arguments for or against progressive education, picking out ideas on both sides of the debate and trying to arrive at a balanced assessment of the question.

FOR

■ *A better understanding of how children learn*

- The Plowden committee sitting in 1965 derived inspiration from Jean Piaget who had discovered that children go through four stages of development, continuing making and remaking their own reality. The committee suggested that there is no point in teaching a child a skill or a concept before he/she is ready for it. It followed that teaching should become child orientated instead of being teacher orientated. Student student interaction should replace student teacher interaction, learning by discovery should replace parrot learning from text-books or teachers' lessons.

■ *Motivating children and creating a friendly classroom*

- In a progressive classroom children are allowed to learn from their mistakes. Teachers are encouraged **to devise** their own lessons. **Fluency** comes before correctness, it is thought too much grammar actually harms pupils'progress.
- Less attention is paid to the curriculum. A friendly supportive atmosphere is created. Learning is made relevant to their background and experience. There is less whole class teaching and **chalk and talk.** There is less teacher student interaction and more and more student student interaction.

■ *Towards a less competitive society*

- Turning schools in competitive place can be damaging to the weaker pupils and those who have been put at disadvantage by a culturally **deprived background** and who will start in life with a low self-esteem. Children learn much better if they are allowed to progress at their own pace.

AGAINST

■ *Has Piaget been misread?*

- The great expectations of the Plowden era have not been fulfilled. It is a fact that a substantial number of pupils leave school without knowing how to read and write properly. Critics of progressive education point an accusing finger to trendy methods and demand a return to basics.

■ *Restoring discipline and a sense of effort at school*

- The belief that children can learn by themselves and through discovery a science or a craft which has taken 2000 years to evolves seems **preposterous** to critics of progressive education. It is only through patient imitation of past masters that painters and writers learned their **trade**. Some **rote learning** is the surest and safest way to learn the basics.
- There are those, like chief Inspector Woodhead who think that **undemanding** and complacent teaching fails to challenge the intelligence of the child and actually hampers his/her progress.

ETHNIC MINORITIES AND RACISM IN THE U.K.

MINORITÉS ETHNIQUES ET RACISME EN G.-B.

FACTSHEET

Immigration from the Caribbean and the South Asian subcontinent dates principally from the 1950s and 1960s. In recent years there has been a rise in immigration from some African countries such as Ghana, Nigeria, Somalia and Uganda.

The 1991 **census** included for the first time a question on ethnic grouping. This found that 94.5% of the population belonged to the 'White' group while over 3 million (5.5%) described themselves as belonging to another ethnic group.

Under 1/2 of the ethnic minority population was born in the U.K. Members of ethnic minority groups were concentrated in industrial and urban areas and over 1/2 lived in the South-East, especially in London.

Although many members of the Black and Asian communities are concentrated in the inner cities, where there are problems of **deprivation** and social stress, many individuals have achieved distinction in their careers and in public life. There are now 9 Black and Asian MPs and the number of ethnic minority councillors in local government is growing. There has also been an expansion of commercial enterprise. Black **competitors** have represented the U.K. in a range of sports (such as athletics, cricket and football) and ethnic minority talents in the arts and in entertainment have been recognised.

Economic, environmental, educational and health programmes of central government and local authorities exist to combat disadvantage. The Commission on the Future of Multi-Ethnic Britain was **set up** in January 1998. It will publish recommendations on how the U.K.'s social and political institutions need to adapt to the changing nature of the population.

Discrimination on grounds of colour, race, nationality, or ethnic or national origin, in the provision of **goods**, **facilities** and services, in employment, in housing, in education and in **advertising** is **unlawful**. It is a criminal **offence** to incite racial **hatred**, and new offences of racial **harassment** and violence and criminal damage were created in 1998.

Urban guerrillas

One autumn afternoon 18 months ago, I was walking across the square in my area of north London.
A little boy was lying on the ground and one of the gang was jumping on his stomach as though it were a mini-trampoline. Others were kicking him all over. His sister was screaming. Two other adults were sitting on benches doing nothing.
Luckily, the black child and his sister were not so badly hurt as to need an ambulance. They **limped off** home very frightened. They were **latchkey children** living on one of the **estates**. They had nowhere to play except the square and another little park across a busy road, which had a **broken-down** playground but which was even more dangerous.

The Sunday Times

Meet the Hindujas

In India, they are known as the Fab Four. Fêted for their munificence and feared for their power, the Hinduja brothers are **household names**. Yet here, despite their friendships with Margaret Thatcher and John Major and the success of their UK businesses and charities, the family has kept a low profile.

That might be about to change.

Yesterday two of the brothers – Srichand, 63, and Gopi, 59 – were revealed to be Britain's richest Asians in a list published by EasternEye newspaper. They are estimated to be worth £1.3 billion, with interests in finance, industry, **oil** and telecommunications. The story of their remarkable rise is a compelling mix of hard work, luck, and suggestions of intrigue and tragedy.

The Guardian

Brooking furious at sport council snub

Trevor Brooking has **threatened** to resign as **stand-in chairman** of the English Sports Council unless he is given the job permanently. The former England **soccer** star has written to the Sports **Secretary** Chris Smith, demanding to know why, after nine months as interim chairman, he has not been appointed on a permanent basis.

The contest for the post has already **propelled** Brooking into a black-versus-white, male-versus-female contest against Tessa Sanderson, gold medal winner in the javelin at the 1984 Olympics.

Smith initially wanted Brooking for the job but his junior **Minister**, Tony Banks, backed Sanderson as part of his personal crusade to get more women and black people into key posts in sports administration.

Smith opted not **to pull rank** and irritate Banks by appointing the double FA Cup winner.

The Observer

The serbian advocate

Marko Gasic, spokesman for the Serbian Information Centre in London.

'I was born in Bradford and came to London when I was four. I am British. But Britain takes on a different **hue** when it is your relatives they are bombing. I am really worried about the **human shields** on the bridge in Belgrade. This week I went on the Today programme. I was tired, I had done three interviews, and wanted to collapse into bed. But Today is important, and I had to go on there to counter Robin Cook's lies.

It's not just a war on the ground, it's a war of propaganda, and Nato have the biggest machine of the lot. Cook said there had been 20 teachers killed in Godan, for example, but Godan is a village of 200 people. They'd be lucky to have one teacher, **let alone** 20.'

The Sunday Times

THÈME

1. Dans les années cinquante et soixante, les citoyens des anciennes colonies, détenteurs de passeports britanniques, ont afflué dans la mère patrie à la recherche d'emplois et d'un meilleur niveau de vie.
2. C'est par le sport ou les médias que de nombreux immigrants de couleur, ou fils ou petits-fils d'immigrants, obtiennent une reconnaissance sociale. Les minorités ethniques ont le droit de voter aux élections parlementaires et municipales, mais il y a encore en Grande-Bretagne peu de députés noirs et asiatiques.
3. En raison de la concentration de la population de couleur dans certains quartiers urbains pauvres, certaines écoles du centre ville ont une majorité d'élèves noirs ou asiatiques, ce qui incite plusieurs parents à envoyer leurs enfants dans des écoles privées.
4. Les divisions sociales se sont aggravées au Royaume-Uni dans les années quatre-vingt avec l'augmentation massive du chômage et les minorités ethniques ont été durement touchées.
5. Même les habitants de couleur qui sont locataires du secteur public se voient attribuer par les municipalités des logements plus vétustes que les Britanniques.
6. Malgré la législation contre la discrimination, il subsiste des comportements racistes et des préjugés dont profitent les groupes d'extrême-droite.
7. Le gouvernement britannique a traditionnellement accordé l'asile à ceux qui fuyaient les persécutions. Beaucoup de ceux qui demandent l'asile semblent maintenant poussés par des facteurs économiques plus que politiques.

VERSION

1. Angry young Asians around Britain may react to the bombing threat with a violent backlash against the white population.
2. West Yorkshire police are deploying extra patrol in Bradford. In Wolverhampton which has a large population of Asians and West Indians, the groups that are responsible for the bombs are causing a lot of panic.
3. Cardiff police are urging people to report any racial incidents.
4. In Glasgow Pakistani Muslim leaders appealed to the city's 21,000 strong ethnic minority population to remain calm.
5. Minorities have long been at risk of isolated attacks against individuals and families. London's carnage shows there is no limit to the outrages those determined enough are willing to perpetrate.
6. Tony Blair believes the forces of decency will defeat intolerance and hate. Jack Straw, the home secretary, rules out the banning of far-right groups in Britain.

1. In the 1950s and 1960s the citizens of former colonies, British passport-holders, flocked to the mother country in search of jobs and a better standard of living.
2. Many coloured immigrants, or sons and grand-sons of immigrants gain social recognition through sport or the media. Ethnic minorities may vote at general and local elections, but there are still few British black and Asian MPs.
3. Owing to the concentration of the coloured population in deprived urban districts, some inner city schools have a majority of black or Asian pupils which causes a number of parents to send their children to private schools.
4. Social divisions worsened in the UK during the 1980s with the dramatic rise of unemployment and ethnic minorities were severely hit.
5. Even those coloured inhabitants who are public sector tenants are allocated by local authorities older housing than white British people.
6. In spite of the anti-discrimination legislation, persistent racist behaviour and prejudice are taken advantage of by far right groups.
7. The British Government has traditionally granted asylum to those fleeing persecutions. Many asylum seekers now seem driven by economic rather than political factors.

1. Il se peut que de jeunes Asiatiques en colère dans toute la Grande-Bretagne réagissent à la menace d'explosions en se retournant violemment contre la population blanche.
2. La police du West Yorkshire déploie des patrouilles supplémentaires à Bradford. A Wolverhampton, qui comporte une importante population d'Asiatiques et d'Antillais, les poseurs de bombes causent une forte panique.
3. La police de Cardiff encourage la population à signaler tout incident racial.
4. A Glasgow, les chefs musulmans pakistanais ont appelé au calme les minorités ethniques qui représentent 21 000 habitants.
5. Les minorités sont depuis longtemps menacées par les attaques isolées contre des individus et des familles. Le carnage de Londres montre que les attentats que les plus résolus sont prêts à commettre ne connaissent pas de limites.
6. Tony Blair croit que les forces morales viendront à bout de l'intolérance et de la haine. Jack Straw, le ministre de l'intérieur, exclut l'interdiction des groupes d'extrême-droite en Grande-Bretagne.

VOCABULARY

advertising .... *publicité*
broken-down .... *délabré*
census .... *recensement*
chairman .... *président*
chunky .... *trapu*
competitors .... *concurrents*
deprivation .... *pauvreté*
estate .... *cité*
facilities .... *équipements*
goods .... *marchandises*
harassment .... *persécution*
hatred .... *haine*
household names .... *tout le monde connaît leur nom*
human shield .... *bouclier humain*
hue .... *nuance*
latchkey children .... *enfants laissés à eux-mêmes*
let alone .... *à plus forte raison*
Minister .... *Secrétaire d'État*
offence .... *délit*
oil .... *pétrole*
Secretary of State .... *ministre*
shield .... *bouclier*
soccer .... *football*
stand in .... *remplaçant*
appoint (to) .... *nommer*
limp off (to) .... *partir en boîtant*
propel (to) .... *propulser*
pull rank (to) .... *abuser de son rang*
resign (to) .... *démissionner*
set up (to) .... *instituer*
slash (to) .... *frapper*
split up (to) .... *diviser*
threaten (to) .... *menacer*
unlawful .... *illégal*

■ Racial abuse is widespread in France as in Britain.
Discrimination particularly in employment is strongly criticised, especially the refusal to promote a coloured person, or unfair dismissal. A few employers still had rather take on a white worker.

■ Immigration has now almost come to an end, except for political asylum.
At the beginning of coloured immigration, ethnic minority workers were considered as giving a positive contribution to the economy. Now it is also believed that they allow cultural diversity. Integration is gradually taking place in spite of tensions, chiefly through sports clubs or associations. There has been a fall in racial violence.

■ By referring to French or English newspapers or magazines, radio or TV broadcasts, find examples of: a) successful Asian or Black immigrants; b) problems with which ethnic minorities are confronted in daily life.
1) Why are coloured people racially abused?
2) Coloured workers are mostly to be found in the textile industry, in transport as bus or taxi drivers, and as hospital nurses or cleaners: a large part is unskilled. Is it the same in France? How can their situation be improved?
3) Cultural differences between the white and coloured population: language, history, religion, way of life. Which are the most important?
4) In which sports can we find coloured champions?
5) Racial violence goes from insults to downright murders. Where can it take place?

THE CHANNEL TUNNEL

LE TUNNEL SOUS LA MANCHE

FACTSHEET

When the **Channel tunnel** connecting Folkestone to Sangatte, near Calais, was inaugurated by the Queen and President Mitterrand on 6 May 1994, a centuries-long dream finally came true. One of the earliest projects was devised in 1802 by an adviser of Napoleon's, and **digging** first began in 1882. So, why did this project succeed when twenty or so others had failed?

The technological and political **breakthrough** was made possible by both technical and political factors. First, a **stratum** of **floodproof blue chalk** running from Folkestone to Calais made it possible to **bore** the tunnel. Secondly, both François Mitterrand and Margaret Thatcher were keen to strengthen their European ties for political and economic reasons respectively.

Two companies won the **bid** to build and **operate** the tunnel:

• TML (Trans-Manche Link), an Anglo-French **consortium**, which was responsible for building the infrastructure.

• Eurotunnel, the **operating company** which in January 1986 was granted a 55-year concession (extended to 99 years in 1999) to **run** all services through the tunnel. The determined leadership of its chairman, Sir Alastair Morton, was a major factor in the successful completion of the project.

The Channel tunnel is the biggest ever **civil engineering** project financed exclusively by private money, with **funding** by 220 banks and 650,000 **shareholders** (500,000 of whom are French). The original budget more than doubled from £4.8bn in November 1987 to £10.5bn in 1994.

The tunnel is 50.45 km long and lies 40 metres below sea level. There are in fact three tunnels: one in each direction and a service tunnel between the two, with 130 cross-passages linking all three tunnels for **maintenance** and **safety** purposes.

The Channel tunnel is used by two types of train: Le Shuttle and Eurostar.

• Le Shuttle runs two services from the terminal near Folkestone to Sangatte: one for private users (cars, coaches and their passengers) and one for **freight** traffic. The **crossing** time is 35 minutes (compared to 75 mins on the fastest ferry **route**).

• Eurostar is a **high-speed** passenger train connecting London Waterloo International to Paris Gare du Nord in 3 hours, and to Brussels Gare du Midi in 2 hours 40 mins. Trains **run** at a maximum speed of 300 km per hour on the continental side and 160 km per hour in the tunnel section (the **crossing** time is 20 minutes). However, they slow down to 100 km per hour on the British side as they run on conventional **tracks**.

There are plans to build a **high-speed track** linking the Channel tunnel to St Pancras Station in London. The line will be used by both international and domestic trains. Work is due to begin in 1999 and should be completed by 2007 under the private sector **consortium** London and Continental Railways Ltd (LCR), which is responsible for the design, construction and ownership of the rail link. This will enable Eurostar trains to link Paris to London in only 2 hours 20 minutes and London to Brussels in 2 hours.

Traffic surges through the tunnel

Eurotunnel carried 20 million people through the **Channel Tunnel** last year, soaring ahead of its rivals with a rise of 10 per cent in passengers travelling between Britain and France [...] while the amount of **freight** carried increased from 6 million to 11 million tonnes. The company now carries more than 50 per cent of the car traffic across the **Channel**. The 1998 figures include 3.35 million cars carried on passenger **shuttle** trains, a 45 per cent increase on the number carried in 1997.

The Guardian

The price war in the **cross-Channel** market is growing in intensity, with the ferry companies maintaining discounts of up to 25 per cent on published prices throughout the summer. Eurotunnel has also offered a number of incentives to customers, including a free day trip after October for those paying a standard or five-day return **fare** and a special overnight return fare of £75-£99. Analysts believe the offers make it even more unlikely Eurotunnel will be able to persuade its banks it can generate enough revenues to pay off its £7.8bn debt.

The Observer (Business Section)

Eurotunnel wins market share from ferry rivals

Eurotunnel has grabbed a big slice of the ferry operators' business on the **cross-Channel** market over the crucial summer months.
Stena Sealink, the second largest ferry company on the Dover-Calais **route**, admitted its passenger volumes fell 10 per cent and **freight** volumes 13 per cent in July compared with the same month last year. These trends have continued during August.

The Observer (Business Section)

Your Eurostar questions answered

There are two classes on board, but both are very comfortable, air-conditioned, and have excellent facilities. Seats are slightly wider, with wider arm rests, in first class, and first class passengers are entitled to a full meal at their seats for no extra charge. [...] Second class passengers can buy snacks and meals from the buffet car or from a trolley which passes along the train. Payment for all purchases can be in English, French or Belgian money, including credit cards.

Top Rail

Eurotunnel's turnover was £666 million, an increase of 26 per cent on 1997. Mr. Ponsolle [the operator's executive chairman] said that these figures hid a debt of £8 billion, which would take years to pay off.

The Guardian

Eurostar. An oncoming train

Eurostar has [reportedly] forced down average airline economy fares by 25-30%. But the real problem for the airlines is that Eurostar has deftly targeted the lucrative business traveller, rather than fighting over cheapskate leisure travellers. Of 794 seats on each Eurostar train, 210 are first class. For journeys between city centres, the train is faster (and more restful) than flying. Eurostar has set its first-class return fares competitively: £220 compared with British A irways' current full fare of £330 for a return trip to Paris.

The Economist

THÈME

1. L'action a déjà gagné près de 40% depuis le début de l'année [1999]. Le titre a profité des premiers bénéfices d'Eurotunnel enregistrés en 1998 et qui ont été annoncés à la mi-mars. Au premier trimestre, les ventes d'Eurotunnel ont grimpé de 18% en raison notamment du niveau record atteint par le transport de marchandises.
2. Mercredi, à la Bourse de Paris, l'action Eurotunnel s'appréciait de 2,02% à 1,51 euro. Selon les projections établies lors de la restructuration financière signée en juillet 1997, les premiers dividendes devraient être versés en 2004.
3. En revanche, ce sont les Britanniques qui paieront les péages : à 70%, le trafic passager à travers la Manche est constitué par les sujets de sa Très Gracieuse Majesté. Et à 8% seulement par les Français.
4. A l'origine le tunnel devait entrer en service au printemps 1993. Puis la date fut remise à l'été. Puis en décembre 1993. Puis au 7 mars 1994. Finalement, ce sera sans doute pour la rentrée prochaine.

VERSION

1. The trains, the **shuttle** and the complex **signalling** in the tunnel proved expensive and difficult to produce, resulting in **delays** prolonged both by the complexity and by escalating **safety** requirements.
2. Why was the **Chunnel** so expensive? There are five main reasons. The divisive nature of Europe; the greed of the construction companies; the demands of the banks; red tape and the scale of the project.
3. The tunnel is the first major Anglo-French collaboration since Concorde - even if it has not been entirely seamless. Ironically, up to 70 per cent of its **users** are likely to be English, and yet nearly 75 per cent of **shareholders** are individual French investors.
4. Each postponement of the opening date has caused Eurotunnel further embarrassment. But the real pain has been financial, since every **delay** has forced Eurotunnel to borrow still more simply to meet the interest burden on its existing debts.
5. [...] Eurotunnel will have raised about £2.5bn from its **shareholders**. Bank borrowings, however, will stand at about £8bn. And with interest payments running at £50m a month, the challenge facing the Tunnel will be to earn sufficient revenues sufficiently quickly to avoid sinking under this sea of debt.
6. It [the Tunnel] is, by any standards, a remarkable engineering achievement, as are the Eurostar trains themselves, capable of working on three different rail systems, taking current from three incompatible power sources.

1. Share values have already increased by almost 40% since the beginning of the year [1999]. The price of shares has benefited from Eurotunnel's first profits chalked up in 1998 and which were announced in the middle of March. In the first quarter, Eurotunnel's sales soared by 18% owing - among other reasons - to the record level of freight traffic.
2. On Wednesday, on the Paris Stock Exchange, Eurotunnel shares rose 2.02 to €1.51. According to the forecasts made when financial restructuring took place in July 1997, the first dividends should be paid in 2004.
3. However, the British will be the main users as they make up 70% of cross-Channel passenger traffic as opposed to only 8% on the French side.
4. Originally the tunnel was due to start operating in the spring of 1993. Then the opening date was put back to the summer. Next, to December 1993. Later, to 7 March 1994. And now there is talk of it being postponed until next autumn.

1. Il s'est avéré coûteux et difficile de réaliser les Eurostar, Le Shuttle et de résoudre les problèmes liés à la signalisation dans le tunnel. Cela a entraîné des retards, encore aggravés du fait de cette complexité et des normes de sécurité toujours plus élevées.
2. Pourquoi le tunnel sous la Manche s'est-il avéré si onéreux ? On peut avancer cinq raisons : les différences qui sèment la discorde au sein de l'Europe, l'appât du gain des entreprises de travaux publics, les exigences des banques, la bureaucratie et l'envergure du projet.
3. Le tunnel représente la collaboration franco-britannique la plus importante depuis le Concorde, même si celle-ci ne s'est pas entièrement déroulée sans heurts. L'ironie du sort, c'est que les Anglais sont susceptibles de représenter environ 70% des usagers, alors que les petits porteurs français constituent 75% des actionnaires.
4. Chaque report de la date d'ouverture a provoqué toujours plus d'embarras pour Eurotunnel. Cependant, là où le bât blesse, c'est sur le plan financier car chaque retard a contraint Eurotunnel à s'endetter encore plus, simplement pour honorer les intérêts sur ses emprunts en cours.
5. [...] Eurotunnel aura collecté 2,5 milliards de livres sterling auprès de ses actionnaires. Cependant, les emprunts contractés auprès des banques s'élèveront à environ 8 milliards de livres sterling. En outre, avec 50 millions de livres en intérêts à rembourser chaque mois, le tunnel devra réussir l'exploit de générer assez rapidement des revenus suffisants pour lui éviter de sombrer dans une mer de dettes.
6. Le tunnel sous la Manche est, de tous les points de vue, une prouesse technologique incontestable, tout comme les Eurostar. Ceux-ci sont capables de circuler sur trois types de rails différents, s'approvisionnant en électricité depuis trois sources incompatibles entre elles.

VOCABULARY

arrival .... *arrivée*
bid .... *appel d'offres, soumission*
blue chalk .... *craie bleue*
book (to)/booking .... *réserver/réservation*
bore (to) .... *percer*
breakthrough .... *percée*
carriage, compartment .... *wagon*
Channel .... *Manche*
Channel tunnel (Chunnel) .... *tunnel sous la Manche*
check in (to) .... *passer à l'enregistrement*
civil engineering .... *génie civil*
consortium .... *consortium*
cross-Channel (adj.) .... *trans-Manche*
crossing .... *traversée*
delay .... *retard*
departure .... *départ*
dig (to) .... *creuser*
dril (to) .... *forer, percer*
fare .... *prix du billet*
floodproof .... *imperméable*
freight/freight train .... *fret/train de marchandises*
funding .... *financement*
go through customs (to) .... *passer la douane*
high-speed (adj.) .... *à grande vitesse*
load (to)/loading .... *charger/chargement*
lorry .... *poids lourd*
maintenance .... *entretien*
make a return journey, a round trip (to) .... *faire un aller retour*
objector, opponent .... *opposant*
operate/operating company .... *exploiter/société d'exploitation*
peak period .... *heure de pointe*
peak season .... *saison touristique*
platform .... *quai*
return ticket .... *billet aller retour*
rolling stock .... *matériel roulant*
route .... *itinéraire, tracé*
run (to) .... *exploiter ; circuler*
safety regulations .... *réglementation en matière de sécurité*
safety standards .... *normes de sécurité*
shareholder .... *actionnaire*
shuttle .... *navette*
signalling .... *signalisation*
single (nom) .... *aller simple (billet)*
spoil .... *déblais*
stratum (plur. strata) .... *couche*
terminal .... *terminal*
track .... *voie*
tunnel boring machine (TBM) .... *tunnelier*
user .... *usager*
work .... *travaux*

The arguments for and against the Channel tunnel

FOR

■ *The economic impact of the tunnel*
- The project led to job creations on both sides of the Channel at a time of high unemployment. For instance, it generated over 5,000 jobs for local people in France, and unemployment in Calais fell from over 20 per cent to less than 14 per cent during the building of the infrastructure.
- The builders placed orders for locomotives, cement, etc. in both countries, thus benefiting a number of French and British companies.

■ *The environmental impact of the tunnel*
- The development of tunnel activities could result in a significant reduction in noise, pollution, road congestion and accidents owing to the use of **freight trains** instead of lorries.

■ *A trouble-free form of Channel-hopping*
- Anyone who has sailed across the Channel in winter will have experienced **delays** due to bad weather, especially when the sea is rough or when there is fog. For tunnel **users**, such problems will be a thing of the past.
- **Loading** times are substantially shorter than with ferries (only 20 minutes).
- Drivers will no longer have to worry about arriving at the port on time as Le Shuttle offers frequent **departures** and advance **booking** is not necessary. It provides a convenient drive-on, drive-off service with passenger services every 15 minutes and **freight** services every 20 minutes at **peak periods**.
- Eurostar takes passengers directly from city centre to city centre.Trains generally **run** on time and the journey is smooth, with up to 28 services in each direction every day. 6.3 million passengers travelled on Eurostar in 1998.
- A price war with the ferries has led to lower **fares**, thus benefiting the customer.

AGAINST

■ *Deep-rooted fears*
- Britain would no longer be an island.
- Some people fear that a potential invader could use the tunnel for military purposes.
- Many British people feel that the tunnel would increase the threat of rabies.
- Some potential travellers are reluctant to use the tunnel because of claustrophobia.
- The tunnel could be used to smuggle drugs into Britain.
- The tunnel provides a potential target for terrorists and saboteurs. For instance, the fire on a **freight train** in November 1996 proved to be an act of sabotage. As a result, services were disrupted till June 1997.

■ *Environmental issues*
- It was difficult to find a site to dispose of the **spoil** without damaging the environment.
- Many environmentalists are opposed to the new rail line in Britain as it will spoil the countryside of Kent, known as the 'Garden of England', and will pass through a densely populated area, thus affecting a large number of people.

■ *Economic factors*
- An estimated 100,000 jobs have been lost in and around the Channel ports, as ferry services have been concentrated in Dover and Calais to the detriment of Folkestone and Boulogne.

Y2K, M-6

AN 2000, M-6

FUTURE AHEAD

FACTSHEET

While the year 2000 is six months away, three new companies – Kodak, Mars and Typhoo Tea – have announced their partnership in the Millennium dome which is being built in Greenwich. Kodak will be exclusively responsible for photography, and Mars for chocolates and sweets. The building company John Laing, **project manager** of the dome – one of the two man-made structures which can be seen from space – has created web sites so that it can be visited virtually:

www. laing. co.uk, www. dome 2000. co.uk or www. panoramic-imaging. ltd.uk.

With or without the year 2,000 the U.K. is a popular resort since the number of tourists increased by 5% during the past three winter months and spending by 7%. The B.T.A. wants to attract still more tourists and it has published a leaflet with quotations from R.L. Stevenson, R. Kipling about the 2000 year old heritage. Photographs of Blenheim castle (where Sir W. Churchill was born), of St Paul's Cathedral or of H.M.S. Victory, Nelson's flagship, illustrate 15 **routes**: Liverpool for instance is both the Beatles city and the harbour to the New World. The British migrants in Australia and Canada are urged to review their **family tree**.

The National Trust will celebrate the Millennium with the ***three master*** Grand Turk, a replica of the 18th century frigate which sailed in a T.V. soap 'Captain Hornblower'. It will sail round the whole of Britain from Ipswich, **taking on board** children from eleven large harbours (including Belfast).

In London the Millennium **pedestrian** bridge is being built between the City and the new Tate Gallery. It is a 4m wide and 350m long **suspension footbridge** over the Thames.

In Dartmoor, the inhabitants of Meavry will dance around the **oak** which is the village's pride and joy, singing Auld Lang Syne. There are over 1,000 very old trees in the country and the **yew tree** in Fortingall, Scotland, is said to be 3,500 years old.

It is silly to say that the majority is always wrong

A study carried out for the Broadcasting Standards Commission – no less – recommended that broadcasters sould drop references to BC and AD in the approach to the Millennium, to avoid offence to other religions. Broadcasters should instead say CE and BCE, meaning the Common Era and Before Common Era. This is silliness almost beyond parody. This country has been Christian for many hundreds of years; it is Christian still. And even if BC and AD do jar with a few members of the ethnic minorities, those people make up only six per cent or less of the entire population; the remaining 94 per cent can hardly be expected to abandon a 2,000-years-old cultural tradition for a very small fraction of that six per cent.

Minette Marrin, The Observer.

The **Uplifting**, the unlikely and the unusual were yesterday highlighted as the greatest innovations for our age when the latest list of Millennium products was announced. Announcing the latest list of 201 products – selected by the Design Council – the Trade and Industry Secretary, Stephen Byers, said: 'Some of the products announced today have earned millions of pounds for UK companies. Others provide solutions to world problems like landmines. It is a truly varied list which reflects the talent and innovation in Britain'.
As well as prestige, the **awards** are likely to have commercial benefits. As well as trumpeting them in advertising, companies will benefit from having their product showcased in the Millennium Dome, expected to be visited by hundreds of thousands – if not millions – of people. They will also be included in travelling exhibitions that will tour internationally.

By Andrew Buncombe, The Independent

Tubby dome bye bye

Worried by the possibility that few adults will feel the urge to trek all the way out beyond Greenwich and then fork out £20 a head to view what looks like being no more than a glorified trade fair financed by a few multinational companies, the NMEC (New Millennium Experience Company) is hoping to persuade the BBC to appeal over the heads of grown ups to the kiddies.
Approaches have even been made to the nation's most cherished cultural icons, the Teletubbies, to introduce the dome as an element in the La-la and co. There is also the hope that the dome may feature prominently in *EastEnders*.
The only **snag** is by the time the thing actually opens, even the kiddies may be bored stiff by the whole idea.

The Observer

Suburban serfs write a new Domesday Book

A few months ago Richard Lynam, a senior partner in an advertising agency who has lived locally for more than 15 years, was in a nearby pub discussing how the community might mark the millennium when he had an inspired idea: rather than a street party we could produce a book, a 'snapshot' of how we live now as a source of interest to local people and lasting record for historians of future generations.
It has become an unexpectedly absorbing project for those of us writing about and photographing our neighbours.
Wouldn't it be interesting, we thought, if people all over Britain were also producing a local record. And it turns out they are – small groups hard at work on books, video diaries, tapestries, tape-recordings and villages maps. The dome is the least of it; the lasting legacy of the millennium may well be a picture of Britain – almost a modern Domesday Book – compiled without any government intervention or encouragement.

Sunday Times

THÈME

1. Le millénaire est l'occasion pour la Grande Bretagne d'accueillir le monde avec une célébration grandiose.
2. Le Dôme à Greenwich occupe deux terrains de football. C'est un fabuleux exemple de la rencontre entre l'ancien et le nouveau.
3. Le thème du Dôme est l'environnement, il représente un investissement de 4 millions de livres dans le cadre d'un partenariat entre le gouvernement et le secteur privé.
4. En dehors du Dôme et dans toute la Grande Bretagne, les gens seront invités à allumer des bougies peu avant minuit le soir du 31 décembre.
5. 10 000 personnes environ seront invitées au Dôme, pour la plupart des citoyens ordinaires, choisis pour leur réussite dans leurs communautés.
6. L'Archevêque de Canterbury fait part depuis plusieurs mois de son inquiétude quant à la cérémonie d'inauguration et à l'absence de participation religieuse.

VERSION

1. Some of Europe's busiest airports and air traffic control centres have fallen seriously behind in their plans to deal with the Millennium bug, the software problem that could bring computers world-wide grinding to a halt at the new year.
2. Experts have predicted chaos and warned that passengers could be at risk. Luton has been **pinpointed** as the British airport giving greatest cause of concern.
3. In the 223 days remaining until **New Year's Eve**, Harvey Goldsmith, the concert promoter, must devise a spectacular event in London capable of appealing to a global television audience as well as entertaining **revellers** on the banks of the Thames.
4. There have been problems raising £5 millions in commercial sponsorship and the police and local authorities have objected to taking responsibility for the safety of **partygoers**.
5. Camelot, the national lottery operator is proposing a new lottery game for Millennium Eve, in which it would create at least 12 millionaires. The game would be shown live shortly after the opening of the Dome.
6. The Dome is not in itself a building at all merely an enclosure for other structures and activities. As these are finished and populated, they will start to give more of a sense of distance and perspective.

1. The Millennium is the opportunity for Britain to welcome people from the whole world with a spectacular celebration.
2. The Greenwich Dome takes up two football grounds; it is a fantastic example of the meeting between the old and the new.
3. The Dome focuses on the environment; it accounts for a £4 million investment in the framework of a partnership between the government and the private sector.
4. Outside the Dome and through out Britain people will be urged to light candles shortly before midnight on New Year's Eve.
5. About 10,000 people will be invited to the Dome, most of them ordinary citizens selected as achievers in their community.
6. The Archbishop of Canterbury has expressed for months his concern about the opening ceremony and its lack of religious involvement.

1. Certains des aéroports et des centres de contrôle de trafic aérien européens les plus actifs ont pris un retard considérable dans leur programme pour faire face au bug de l'an 2000, le problème de logiciel qui pourrait bloquer tous les ordinateurs du monde au nouvel an.
2. Les experts ont prédit le chaos et averti que les passagers pourraient être menacés ; ils ont indiqué que Luton est l'aéroport britannique le plus inquiétant.
3. Dans les 223 jours qui nous séparent de la Saint Sylvestre, H. Goldsmith, l'organisateur de concerts, doit imaginer un événement spectaculaire à Londres susceptible de plaire à un public de télévision global et en même temps de distraire les fêtards sur les rives de la Tamise.
4. Il a été difficile de réunir 5 millions de livres en sponsorat commercial et les municipalités se sont refusées à accepter la responsabilité de la sécurité des fêtards.
5. Camelot, la compagnie de la loterie nationale propose un nouveau jeu pour la Saint Sylvestre 1999, qui ferait au moins 12 millionnaires. Le jeu serait diffusé en direct peu après l'inauguration du Dôme.
6. Le Dôme en lui-même n'est absolument pas un bâtiment, seulement une enceinte pour d'autres structures et activités. Au fur et à mesure que celles-ci seront achevées et peuplées, elles commenceront à donner un plus grand sens de la distance et de la perspective.

VOCABULARY

award .... *prix*
barge .... *péniche*
family tree .... *arbre généalogique*
flagship .... *vaisseau amiral*
New Year's Eve .... *St Sylvestre*
oak .... *chêne*
pedestrian .... *piéton*
project manager .... *maître d'œuvre*
pin point (to) .... *indiquer*
remnant .... *reste*
revellers, partygoers .... *fêtards*
route .... *itinéraire*
snag .... *inconvénient*
soap .... *feuilleton*
standards .... *normes*
show live (to) .... *diffuser en direct*
suspension footbridge .... *passerelle suspendue*
three-master .... *trois mâts*
take on board (to) .... *embarquer*
jar with (to) .... *ne pas s'accorder avec*
uplifting .... *tonique*
yew tree .... *if*

Topic for discussion

Where would you like to be on the eve of the Millennium?

■ Ideas for research:
What would you include among the greatest innovations of our age? Could you produce a local record?

Elements for debate:

FOR

■ Good points of the Millennium:
- for tourism in Britain - in the field of employment;
- for the improvement of the environment;
- for the monarchy and the Prime Minister who will take part in celebrations;
- for British industry: the inclusion of products in the list is going to let people know about them;
- for architect Richard Rogers who designed the Dome and for the Alsop firm responsible for North Greenwich Tube Station.

AGAINST

■ Disadvantages of the Millennium:
- for computer-run systems which regulate air or rail traffic;
- for local authorities who have to organise celebrations in London;
- for the Church because Christmas will be overshadowed by New Year's Eve.

THE POWER OF THE PRESS IN THE USA

LE POUVOIR DE LA PRESSE AUX ÉTATS-UNIS

FACTSHEET

If the American press, often referred to as '**the Fourth Estate**', has the power to counterbalance the government, it is thanks to the First Amendment to the American Constitution, which guarantees 'free speech' and 'the freedom of the press'.

In fact, this right to inform may be restricted in the name of national security, and the government has tried to influence public opinion in particular concerning war since Vietnam. Yet a free press has become such an essential feature of American society that every attempt by the government to control it only reasserted the independence of investigative journalism.

During the Vietnam War (from 1963 to 1975), the press started denouncing the 'credibility gap' while President Johnson was in power (1963-1968), accusing the government of releasing **biased information** and half-truths in order to manipulate both the press and public opinion.

During Richard Nixon's presidency (1968-1974), two events established the power and independence of the press:

1- The PENTAGON PAPERS: in June 1971, Daniel Ellsberg, an ex-Defense Department employee, released a secret Defense Department history of the Vietnam War which was published by ***The New York Times*** in order to bring the war to an end. President Nixon sued the paper in the name of national interest but when ***The NYT*** was forced to suspend the publication of the documents ***The Washington Post*** carried on with it, then ***The Boston Globe,*** etc., until the Supreme Court proved the press right.

2- WATERGATE: 'Watergate' is the name of a Washington building in which the Democratic Party had its headquarters and which was tapped and spied on by President Nixon's Republican Party. The term refers to the whole scandal that was then **exposed**, from illegal campaign practices to the President's perjury to cover up the whole affair. The investigation, led by two reporters from ***The Washington Post*** (Bob Woodward and Carl Bernstein), led to the President's resignation on August 9, 1974.

Thus Watergate, which marked a turning point in the history of investigative journalism and reinforced both the American people's distrust of government and the power of the press, has become a set phrase used to refer to later scandals, from 'Irangate' to 'Monicagate':

– IRANGATE: in November 1986, during Ronald Reagan's presidency (1984-1992), the press revealed that the USA had sold arms illegally to Iran, first to free the American hostages held in Beirut, then to support the guerilla war in Nicaragua (hence the expression of 'Iran-Contra' scandal). The President remained in power by shifting responsibility to a few top army officials who had to resign.

– THE CLINTON YEARS: Before Bill Clinton was elected President in November 1992, the scandal of WHITEWATER was revealed by ***The New York Times*** in March 1992: it seemed that Bill and Hillary Clinton had been involved in a real estate deal, in Arkansas, back in 1978 when Bill Clinton was Attorney General, which led to a fraudulent bankruptcy. In June 1993, after a 4-month inquiry Judge Robert Fiske cleared the Clintons in the case, but in September 1993, a new judge was appointed: Kenneth Starr. The judge, a Republican and religious conservative, was to work on the case for several years, but no decisive element was added to the Whitewater inquiry. Yet Kenneth Starr looked into Bill Clinton's reputation of a womanizer and a first scandal hit the President with Paula Jones' accusations of sexual harassment, dating back to the time when he was Governor of Arkansas. The case was eventually dismissed in Court but in the meantime a bigger scandal **hit the headlines** of all American newspapers in January 1998: **MONICA LEWINSKY**, an ex-White House intern had revealed she had had an affair with the President.The press covered the scandal in such detail for over a year that public opinion supported the President who was perceived as the victim of muckraking journalism, thus marking a 'divorce' between the Americans and a 'Puritan' press.

Don't Blame the Press For a Job It Had to Do

The president told one of the biggest, fattest lies in history, but the public wants to impeach the press. (...) If the president had told the truth immediately, the story would have died. But it is our job to undo the spin and look into the lies and go the extra skeptical mile to see that there is no cover-up. (...)
The impure history of American government – Vietnam, Watergate, Iran-contra – proves that reporters have a duty to dig the truth, whatever the public thinks. Next time, it may not be about sex and lies. It may be about life and death.

The New York Times

The New Journalism Ethic: 'Just the Forecasts, Ma'am'

In effect, reporters have become what weather forecasters always were: predictors. (...) Beside the fact that predictive news is often wrong, what's corrosive, and maddening, about this trend is that it introduces a filter of superiority into news coverage that turns off readers. (...) If reporters feel that the who, what, when and where of most stories have already been covered by the time they file, then the way to attract audience – and respect – is to speculate less on the whatnots future and focus more on the hows and whys of the moment.

The New York Times

For Pentagon Censors, An Easy Victory, Too

In the Gulf war, however, although it was clearly a less challenging episode than World War II and Vietnam, the military went further than ever in order to control information. Not only did stories have to be cleared before publication or airing; reporters and cameras were limited in their movements, and inadequate 'pool' coverage was the rule. Even troop interviews were monitored and sometimes forbidden. (...)
Thus was the First Amendment badly wounded in Desert Storm, although war-giddy Americans seemed not to know about or mourn this national casualty.

The New York Times

THÈME

1. Ce journal à scandales a déjà été poursuivi pour diffamation plusieurs fois.
2. Les changements de la vie sociale et économique pourraient expliquer le nombre décroissant de lecteurs, particulièrement chez les jeunes.
3. Dans le numéro de la semaine dernière, le magazine a publié un reportage intitulé : l'***Infospectacle***.
4. En 1971, le ***New York Times*** commença à publier une série d'articles sur la guerre du Vietnam, au mépris des souhaits exprimés par le gouvernement de Richard Nixon.
5. De plus en plus de journaux sont sous le contrôle d'un nombre de groupes de presse de plus en plus réduit.
6. En moyenne, le prix des quotidiens aux États-Unis varie entre 25 et 60 cents.
7. Aux États-Unis, très peu de quotidiens sont distribués à travers tout le pays, et la plupart des lecteurs sont informés par la presse locale.
8. Les magnats de la presse ne sont pas un phénomène récent aux États-Unis mais ces groupes puissants peuvent représenter une menace pour l'indépendance de la presse, à travers la publicité, essentielle à la survie économique d'un journal.

VERSION

1. Polls showed that the American public, by a wide margin, approved of this drastic information control.
2. Nor did press and television protest as effectively as they should have, that much of what they conveyed was not only controlled by the military but prettified for home consumption.
3. Once the Gulf War was over, the US Air Force chose **to disclose** facts that few newspaper readers could have suspected while the fighting was going on.
4. Over the last thirty years there has been a steady decline in the trust Americans have in their media. Among many sins, they stand accused of being manipulated, of mongering scandals, while true investigative journalism is dying.
5. The press is no longer able to draw lines because competition ensures that any scandal will eventually find someone to publish it.
6. The **chief editor** hoped that the controversy would ultimately translate into more advertising and circulation revenue.

1. This tabloid has already been sued for libel several times.
2. Changes in social and economic life may account for the declining readership, especially among the young.
3. In last week's issue, the magazine ran a report headlined INFOTAINMENT.
4. In 1971, ***The New York Times*** began to publish a series of articles/reports on the Vietnam War, in defiance of the Richard Nixon administration's wishes.
5. More and more papers are controlled by fewer and fewer newsgroups.
6. On average, dailies in the USA are priced between 25 and 60 cents.
7. In the USA, very few dailies are distributed nationwide, and most readers get informed by local papers.
8. Press magnates/barons are no recent phenomenon in the USA but these powerful groups may represent a threat to the independence of the press through advertising, essential to the economic survival of a paper.

1. Les sondages ont montré que le public américain, dans sa grande majorité, approuvait ce contrôle sévère de l'information.
2. La presse et la télévision n'ont pas non plus protesté aussi efficacement qu'elles l'auraient dû, pour dénoncer le fait qu'une grande partie de ce qu'elles transmettaient n'était pas seulement contrôlé par l'armée mais arrangé, enjolivé pour la consommation familiale.
3. Une fois la guerre du Golfe terminée, l'armée de l'air américaine choisit de révéler des faits que peu de lecteurs auraient pu imaginer pendant que les combats avaient lieu.
4. Ces trente dernières années ont vu une baisse régulière de la confiance que les Américains font à leurs médias. Entre autres nombreux péchés, on leur reproche d'être manipulés, de vendre du scandale, pendant que le véritable journalisme d'investigation se meurt.
5. La presse n'est plus en mesure de se fixer des limites parce que la pression de la concurrence assure finalement de la publication de n'importe quel scandale.
6. Le rédacteur en chef espérait que la controverse se traduirait finalement par davantage de bénéfices liés à la publicité et à la distribution.

VOCABULARY

print journalism	*la presse écrite*
a daily (newspaper)	*un quotidien*
a weekly (magazine)	*un hebdomadaire*
a monthly	*un mensuel*
a (medical/technical) journal	*une revue spécialisée*
a copy	*un exemplaire*
an issue	*un numéro*
the circulation	*le tirage*
the readership	*le lectorat/les lecteurs*
a subscription	*un abonnement*
a broadsheet	*un journal de qualité (grand format)*
a tabloid	*un journal à scandales (demi-format)*
a rag	*une "feuille de chou"*
the gutter press/the yellow press	*la presse à scandales*
an editor/a chief editor	*un rédacteur/rédacteur en chef*
a newspaperman/woman	*un journaliste de la presse écrite*
a columnist	*un chroniqueur*
a column	*une chronique*
a photograph/a picture	*une photo*
a photographer	*un photographe*
photography	*(l'art de) la photographie*
a headline	*un gros titre*
a subhead(ing)	*un sous-titre*
hit the headlines (to)	*faire les gros titres*
the front page	*la une*
the lead story	*l'article à la une*
a leader/an editorial	*un éditorial*
a leading article	*un éditorial*
a cover story	*un article en couverture*
the news (is)	*les nouvelles*
current events	*l'actualité*
a news item	*une information/un fait divers*
a press cutting/clipping	*une coupure de presse*
information	*l'information/les informations*
journalese	*le jargon journalistique*
a critic	*un critique*
a film/book review	*une critique de film/livre*
review a film/book (to)	*faire la critique d'un film*
biased/unbiased	*partial/impartial*
dependable/reliable	*fiable*
libel (to)	*diffamer*
libel	*diffamation*
censor (to)	*censurer*
censorship	*la censure*
expose (to)/disclose (to)	*révéler*
the Fourth Estate	*le 4e pouvoir*
media coverage	*couverture médiatique*
a press baron/magnate	*un magnat de la presse*
run a paper (to)	*diriger un journal*
hold a press conference (to)	*tenir une conférence de presse*

The power of the press in perspective

■ Toward 'fast-food' information?

- The second largest circulation for a national paper (after ***The Wall Street Journal***) is ***USA Today,*** with a readership of about 1.6 million a day. This daily was launched in 1982 by the first newsgroup in the USA (Gannett), and it certainly marked the beginning of a new trend: ***USA Today*** is often referred to as 'McPaper' - after McDonald's restaurants - for its fast-information style. Indeed, the paper insists on *facts* rather than analysis, and favours 'optimistic' news, presented with big headlines, photos in colour, short and easy-to-read articles. Most Americans do not recognize themselves in the elitist and mostly political analyses of such papers as ***The New York Times*** or ***The Washington Post***, which view the USA from a 'limited' angle. Of course this may well account for the limited impact of the virulent articles against President Clinton concerning the Monica Lewinsky scandal.

■ The freedom of the press vs economic criteria

- The American press has undergone a major evolution in the past 50 years, as the economic pressure of competition has reduced the number of independent dailies. This phenomenon of 'consolidation' means that today five big groups control one third of the circulation of daily newspapers, which in itself represents a threat to the freedom of the press. Thus in 97% of American towns, local papers have no competitor, which reduces the notion of 'debate'.
- The sources of information today are certainly more diverse than even 30 years ago, but economic factors such as advertising weigh on the independence of journalists: the low price (hence the circulation) of papers largely depends on corporate support.
- Both consolidation and advertising stress that papers have become a mere commodity (= a product) and that the press must *sell* to survive. This may account for the 'tabloidization' of many papers, and the shift from investigative and political journalism toward muckraking journalism, developing what is often called 'Infotainment' (= Information- Entertainment).

■ The press and I.T. (= Information Technology)

- On the one hand, new technologies such as the Internet bring more diversity of opinion and information - therefore more freedom of information - to Americans. Web sites allow more freedom of expression for interest groups (= lobbies) thus reinforcing some form of direct democracy, yet some racist, anti-abortion sites have also shown their dangerous impact. The notion of 'free expression' can be questioned in such cases, and the case of the 'Nuremberg Files', an anti-abortion site which published personal information about doctors practising abortions were considered close to a call to murder, and several lawsuits opposed the First Amendment to the Fourth one, which guarantees the right to privacy. So it seems that these new media, like the traditional press, can both protect or jeopardize (= endanger) democracy.

L'EUTHANASIE : UN SUJET CONTROVERSÉ

EUTHANASIA: A CONTROVERSIAL ISSUE

FACTSHEET

Au cours de ce siècle, un constant émerveillement a accompagné les progrès d'une médecine qui a permis de délivrer l'homme de bien des maux et d'accroître son espérance de vie : celle-ci a augmenté d'un tiers depuis 1960 et dépasse 70 ans dans trente pays.
Toutefois, si l'opinion publique sait gré à la médecine d'allonger la durée de vie, elle lui demande aussi d'adoucir la mort – qualité de vie ne pouvant plus être dissociée de qualité de mort. L'attente des patients n'est certes pas nouvelle car dès 1605 le philosophe anglais Francis Bacon forgea le terme **d'euthanasie** qui signifie "bonne mort, mort douce et sans souffrance" (Littré).

Mais si l'euthanasie suscite aujourd'hui un tel débat c'est qu'elle consiste souvent, non seulement à laisser mourir, mais à provoquer la mort d'une personne. Nombre de médecins s'affranchissent des directives de l'Ordre et des impératifs inscrits dans **le Serment d'Hippocrate** ('I will give no deadly medicine to any one if asked, nor suggest any such counsel') et pratiquent clandestinement l'euthanasie. C'est ainsi qu'en 1936 Lord Dawson **mit fin** aux jours du roi George VI. Certains, néanmoins, à l'instar du docteur américain Jack Kevorkian – alias Doctor Death – n'hésitent plus à donner toute la publicité qu'ils estiment nécessaire à la défense de leur cause. Ils savent pouvoir en effet compter sur le soutien grandissant de l'opinion qui, dans un sondage conduit en 1996 aux États-Unis se montra favorable à 39% à l'action de Kevorkian, et opposée à 41% à une interdiction gouvernementale du **suicide assisté**. Il en va de même en Grande-Bretagne où 86% des personnes interrogées estiment que l'euthanasie devrait être légalisée dans le cas de patients atteints de **maladies incurables**. A l'évidence, si les autorités, dans la plupart des pays, rejettent l'institutionnalisation de cette "mort douce", elles tendent fréquemment au travers de leur système judiciaire à faire preuve d'une attitude plus compréhensive dont se félicitent les associations de défense du "**droit de mourir** dans la dignité". En tout état de cause, au-delà de ses aspects purement techniques et médicaux, l'euthanasie soulève de difficiles questions d'ordre moral et légal.

Pour l'heure, dans l'attente d'une hypothétique législation sur le sujet, un nombre croissant de personnes prennent leurs dispositions afin de ne pas être **maintenues en vie** contre leur gré. Par exemple, elles stipulent dans un "**testament de vie**" leur refus de tout **acharnement thérapeutique**. Dans le même esprit existent des bracelets où sont gravés les mots "**Ne pas réanimer**". Des livres conseillent également leurs lecteurs sur les moyens les plus pratiques de **pratiquer** une euthanasie, qualifiée d'**active** ou **passive, volontaire** etc. Les partisans de "mort douce" se regroupent enfin au sein d'associations qui, aux États-Unis surtout, contestent en justice la constitutionnalité des lois sur l'aide au suicide, et s'expriment avec ferveur sur le Web.

Many Turning to Internet for Aid with Suicide

The Last Rights Information Center includes the text of major court rulings on the subject, including a decision by the 2nd U.S. Circuit Court of Appeals, in New York, which struck down New York's law against **assisted suicide** in April.

There is also Life's End, an on-line shopping center that provides information on things like insurance, imported Italian urns and handmade coffins and a Garden of Remembrance page for obituary notices.

DeathNet has recorded 169,000 visits by computer users since it was set up. 'However they hear of us, they still have to send us their medical records and come there for a consultation,' Kevorkian said last weekend.

Although Kevorkian may be on the cutting edge of end-to-life medicine, he is anything but a World Wide Web wizard. 'It doesn't interest me,' said Kevorkian, a 67-year-old pathologist.

Jack Lessenberry/The New York Times

Suicide Bans are Constitutional, Says Supreme Court

The state has an interest in protecting vulnerable groups including the poor, the elderly and **disabled** people from abuse, neglect and mistakes. The court of appeals dismissed the state's concern that disadvantaged people might be pressured into physician-**assisted suicide** as 'ludicrous on its face'. We have recognized, however, the real risk of subtle coercion and undue influence in end-of-life situations.

The state's interest here goes beyond protecting the vulnerable from coercion; it extends to protecting disabled and **terminally ill** people from prejudice, negative and inaccurate stereotypes and 'societal indifference'. The state's assisted-suicide ban reflects and reinforces its policy that the lives of terminally ill, disabled and elderly people must be no less valued than the lives of the young and healthy and that a seriously disabled person's suicidal impulses should be interpreted and treated the same way as anyone else's.

Finally, the state may fear that permitting assisted suicide will start it down the path to **voluntary** and perhaps even **involuntary euthanasia**.

Chief Justice Rehnquist/The New York Times

Euthanasia in the Netherlands

The Netherlands is the only country in the world where euthanasia is openly **practised**. It is not allowed by statute, but the law accepts a standard defence from doctors that have adhered to official guidelines. These hinge on voluntariness of the request and unrelievable-ness of the suffering. In practice, citizens of other countries are not eligible for euthanasia in the Netherlands. Euthanasia is popularly taken to mean any form of termination of life by a doctor. The definition under Dutch law, however, is narrower. It means the termination of life by a doctor at the express **wish** of a patient. The request to the doctor must be voluntary, explicit and carefully considered and it must have been made repeatedly. Moreover, the patient's **suffering** must be **unbearable** and without any prospect of improvement. Pain relief administered by a doctor may shorten a patient's life. As is the case in other countries, this is seen as a normal medical decision in terminal care and not as euthanasia.

Chris Docker/Glossary of the Scottish Voluntary Euthanasia Society

EXTRA!!! CLASSI-FILES EXTRA!!!

THÈME

1. Dans la vie de chacun, arrive un moment où la mort ne peut plus être repoussée, quelques soient les moyens utilisés. Il s'ensuit qu'il n'y a pas de nécessité morale ni médicale à ce que tous les traitements possibles soient administrés à un patient ni que la vie soit préservée à tout prix.
2. L'euthanasie est actuellement sujet à débat dans un grand nombre de démocraties occidentales. Des études récentes montrent que la plupart des gens y sont favorables. Aux États-Unis, 80 pour cent ont déclaré qu'ils ne voudraient pas voir leur vie prolongée par acharnement thérapeutique, et dans certains pays ce n'est plus un délit d'aider au suicide d'un patient, à la condition qu'il ait clairement exprimé son souhait.
3. Un patient est dans un lit d'hôpital, incapable de bouger, relié à des appareils qui le maintiennent en vie. Il souffre terriblement. Il supplie ses médecins de débrancher tous ces appareils afin qu'il puisse mourir en paix. Mais s'ils refusent parce que les éteindre va à l'encontre de leur éthique, le patient n'a-t-il pas le droit de prendre cette décision et désigner un ami ou membre de sa famille qui veillera à ce qu'il ne soit pas maintenu en vie contre son gré ?
4. Alors que la plupart des gens, effrayés à la perspective d'être maintenus en vie, sans espoir de guérison, pendant des mois, voire des années, disent qu'ils préféreraient demander l'arrêt de tout traitement, nous pouvons nous interroger pour savoir qui doit assumer le poids de cette décision. De fait, administrateurs d'hôpitaux, médecins, membres des familles, et éventuellement les patients eux-mêmes seront tous nécessairement confrontés à l'euthanasie.
5. La question est de savoir s'il existe un "droit de mourir", c'est-à-dire d'avoir la maîtrise de sa propre mort, ou en d'autres termes de choisir une mort humaine et digne. Cependant beaucoup pensent que les gouvernements ne devraient pas légaliser l'euthanasie, mais en laisser la décision à chaque médecin, selon sa conscience.

EXTRA!!! CLASSI-FILES EXTRA!!!

VERSION

1. Doctors are allowed to resort to euthanasia only if there is no alternative – such as **palliative care** of **terminally ill** patients. However research published in the Journal of Medical Ethics claims doctors in the Netherlands – where **voluntary euthanasia** has been decriminalised since 1984 – are ignoring guidelines intended to protect patients. *The Guardian*
2. Euthanasia can only be **carried out** at the patient's explicit request and when there is **intolerable suffering** without prospect of improvement. Those who breach rules can be charged with murder. The survey found out that of the 4,500 cases in 1995 where medics admitted they intentionally terminated life, 900 patients had not explicitly stated they wanted euthanasia. *The Guardian Weekly*
3. How we die, including whether or not we legalize euthanasia, is not just a private, individual decision, as those who are pro-euthanasia argue, it is also an issue that concerns the whole of society. But there is confusion in the definition of euthanasia. Some of this confusion is accidental, some is deliberate as part of political tactic to promote the legalization of euthanasia. *Dr. M. Somerville /McGill University Ethics and Law Journal*
4. In an interview, Derek Humphry, author of 'Final Exit', a how-to book on suicide, said: 'As to helping people to die via Internet, yes, I do that whenever necessary.' For years, people interested in planned death found one another only with great difficulty, mostly through word of mouth. But on Jan. 10, 1995, Hofsess, a former film critic who lives in Vancouver, British Columbia, began DeathNet on the World Wide Web. *The New York Times*

1. There is a point in everyone's life when death can no longer be held off, no matter what means are used. Therefore, it is not morally nor medically required that every possible treatment be given a patient nor that life be preserved at all costs.
2. Euthanasia is currently an issue in many Western democracies. Recent surveys show that most people are in favour of it. In the US, 80 per cent said they would not want their lives prolonged by useless medical treatment and in some countries it is no longer a crime to assist in the suicide of a patient, providing he or she has clearly stated his or her wish.
3. A patient is in a hospital bed, unable to move, attached to life-sustaining equipment. He is in terrible pain. He begs his doctors to disconnect all those machines so that he can die in peace. But if they refuse because it goes against their code of conduct, doesn't the patient have a right to make that decision and designate a friend or family member who will see to it that he is not kept alive against his will?
4. When most people – frightened at the prospect of being kept alive for months, even years without any hope of recovery – say that they would prefer to have treatment withheld, we can ask ourselves who is to bear the burden of the decision. As a matter of fact, hospital administrators, doctors, family members and possibly the patients themselves will all have to face euthanasia.
5. The question is whether there is a 'right to die', namely to have control over one's own death, or in other words choose a humane, dignified death. However, many people think governments should not legalise euthanasia but leave the decision to the conscience of individual physicians.

1. Les médecins sont autorisés à recourir à l'euthanasie uniquement s'il n'y a pas d'autre solution – telle que les soins palliatifs pour des patients en phase terminale. Cependant, d'après un travail de recherche publié dans le Journal d'Éthique Médicale, il apparaîtrait qu'aux Pays-Bas – où l'euthanasie est dépénalisée depuis 1984 – les praticiens ne tiennent pas compte des directives visant à protéger les patients.
2. L'euthanasie ne peut être pratiquée qu'à la demande explicite du patient et dans le cas d'une souffrance intolérable sans perspective d'amélioration. Ceux qui enfreignent les règlements peuvent se voir inculpés de meurtre. L'étude a révélé qu'en 1995, sur les 4.500 cas où des toubibs ont reconnu avoir délibérément mis un terme à des vies, 900 patients n'avaient pas exprimé explicitement leur désir d'euthanasie.
3. La manière dont nous mourons, qui inclut la question d'une légalisation ou non de l'euthanasie, ne se réduit pas à une décision privée, personnelle, comme le soutiennent les partisans de l'euthanasie ; c'est également un problème qui concerne l'ensemble de la société. Mais il existe une confusion dans la définition de l'euthanasie. Cette confusion est en partie accidentelle, et pour une part délibérée en tant qu'elle relève d'une tactique politique visant à promouvoir l'euthanasie.
4. Derek Humphry, auteur de *Exit final : pour une mort dans la dignité*, un manuel sur le suicide, s'est exprimé ainsi, lors d'une interview : "Quant à aider les gens à mourir via l'Internet, oui, je le fais chaque fois que c'est nécessaire". Pendant des années, les gens intéressés par la mort planifiée ne se retrouvaient qu'avec grande difficulté, essentiellement par le bouche à oreille. Mais le 10 janvier 1995, Hofsess, ancien critique de cinéma qui réside à Vancouver en Colombie britannique, a lancé DeathNet sur le Web.

VOCABULARY

active/passive euthanasia	*l'euthanasie active/passive*
aid (to)/assist a suicide (to)	*aider à un suicide*
alleviate (to)/ease suffering (to)	*alléger les souffrances*
Alzheimer's disease	*la maladie d'Alzheimer*
brain damage	*lésions cérébrales*
brain death	*la mort cérébrale*
be in a coma (to)	*être dans le coma*
cure (to)/a cure	*guérir/un remède*
degrading	*dégradant*
be dependent on (to)/dependency	*être dépendant de/la dépendance*
sb's desire/wish to die	*le désir/souhait de qq de mourir*
be disabled (to)	*être handicapé*
(doctor-) assisted suicide	*le suicide (médicalement) assisté*
a fatal disease	*une maladie mortelle*
be force-fed (to)	*être alimenté de force*
hasten (to)/induce death (to)	*précipiter/provoquer la mort*
the Hippocratic oath	*le serment d'Hippocrate*
a hopeless case	*un cas désespéré*
be incapacitated (to)	*être invalide*
incurable	*incurable*
inject sb with sth (to)	*faire à qq une piqûre de qqch*
be kept alive artificially (to)	*être maintenu en vie artificiellement*
a living will	*un testament de vie (ou biologique)*
look after oneself (to)	*se débrouiller tout seul*
be in (to)/suffer (great) pain (to)	*souffrir (beaucoup)*
be paralysed (to)	*être paralysé*
practise (to)/carry out euthanasia (to)	*pratiquer l'euthanasie*
prescribe death-inducing drugs (to)	*prescrire des médicaments qui entraînent la mort*
pro-choice/pro-life	*favorable/opposé à l'euthanasie*
prolong life (to)	*prolonger la vie*
quadraplegic	*tétraplégique*
recovery	*la guérison*
regain consciousness (to)	*reprendre conscience*
do not resuscitate	*ne pas réanimer*
the right to die	*le droit de mourir*
stop (to)/withhold treatment (to)	*arrêter/mettre fin au traitement*
sb's suffering	*la souffrance de qq*
take one's (own) life (to)	*mettre fin à ses jours*
be taken off a machine (to)	*ne plus être relié à un appareil*
be terminally ill (to)	*être en phase terminale*
unbearable/intolerable	*insupportable/intolérable*
useless medical treatment	*l'acharnement thérapeutique*
a vegetable	*un légume*
be in a vegetative state (to)	*être dans un état végétatif*
voluntary/involuntary euthanasia	*l'euthanasie volontaire (voulue) /involontaire (non voulue)*

The pros and cons of euthanasia

FOR: The advocates of euthanasia (pro-choice arguments)

■ *The medical aspect*
- Thanks to medical progress, there are more elderly people, many of whom will be affected by Alzheimer's disease.
- Advances in medicine keep severely disabled or seriously ill people alive longer.

■ *The moral aspect*
- Everyone has a right to determine when and how they will die. On all public opinion polls, most people are in favour of it.
- Many patients feel they are stripped of their dignity when they are totally dependent on machines/when they are left to suffer for months/when they are treated as guinea-pigs.

■ *The legal aspect*
- Laws should be passed to legalise euthanasia.
- Different forms of euthanasia can be clearly defined: active euthanasia (inducing death by use of drugs with the aid of a doctor or any other person); passive euthanasia (stopping treatment); assisted suicide (assisting another person to end his or her life at that person's explicit wish); voluntary euthanasia (the person clearly states their wish to die); involuntary euthanasia (also called mercy killing, ending somebody's life without their consent).
- Different documents enable you to express your wish: living will (a written document in which a person states that he or she doesn't want to be kept alive artificially); alert card (a small card that alerts people to the fact that you've made a living will); 'Do not resuscitate' bracelet (you can wear it to alert people).

AGAINST: The opponents to euthanasia (pro-life arguments)

■ *The medical aspect*
- A doctor's role is to cure, not kill patients. (The Hippocratic oath)
- In the near future, thanks to medical progress, a number of people will certainly be cured of diseases that are still fatal today.
- Medical students should receive training in pain relief treatment and palliative medicine.

■ *The moral aspect*
- Euthanasia is nothing but a murder.
- Human life is sacred/The advocates of euthanasia have no respect for the sanctity of life / No one can decide that his or her life, or anyone's is not worth living.
- It's a slippery slope: once legalisation is obtained, abuse will follow – euthanasia will be used by some to get rid of 'inferior' people, or maybe people's lives will be terminated in exchange for money.
- Man is God's creature: human beings have no right to take their own lives.

■ *The legal aspect*
- The state, whose role is to protect vulnerable people from criminal attempts or suicidal impulses, must ban all forms of euthanasia.
- The decision to induce death is not only a personal one, but also concerns society itself.

CHILD LABOUR

LE TRAVAIL DES ENFANTS

FACTSHEET

It is a widely recognised and publicised shame that our world is going into the 21st century with child labour still an unresolved social issue.

Altogether 250 million children, as young as five years old, are reported to work all over the world, often more than 10 hours a day, in **appalling conditions**. For unscrupulous employers, they are a source of cheap and obedient workers.

Child labour is a widespread **scourge** in developing countries, but also exists in developed countries: **one out of five** children in Asia and Latin America, one out of three in Africa. Their work ranges from unpaid labour within the family to the cruelest form of exploitation in **sweatshops** or **brothels**.

Many children work in agriculture or fishing. In Brazil an estimated three million child labourers work on plantations and in the US as many as 800,000 children under the age of 16 are employed as seasonal and **migrant farmworkers**. In large cities, they can also be found in the manufacturing and **service industry** (factory workers, waiters, hotel maids,…).

Still worse is **bonded labour**, quite common in India, Nepal or Pakistan. Children are in fact sold into servitude in exchange for a loan or a cash advance. If the families are unable to pay their debt back, the children are trapped in many years, or even a lifetime, of **slavery**. Far from home, child slaves are forced to work beyond their physical capacity, and often locked up and subjected to extreme **physical abuse**. Many work in sweatshops producing sports shoes, clothes, or weaving carpets by hand. In Persian Gulf States young Bangladeshi boys are deliberately underfed to be used as camel jockeys. A less documented form of child exploitation is domestic work. Young girls are employed as domestic servants by families who have 'adopted' them. Invisible because they stay indoors, they often fall victim to physical and sexual abuse.

It is in **the sex industry** that child exploitation is the grimmest. Children are **abducted** or **lured into following** recruiting agents who promise them money or a job. They are then smuggled into another country to **be sold into prostitution**. Thailand has been widely criticised for **turning a blind eye to** child **sex workers**.

Working children face safety and health risks as they are often underfed or exposed to toxic chemicals. Child prostitutes are likely to be **HIV positive** or contract other **STDs** (sexually transmitted diseases).

Dire poverty and lack of educational opportunities explain this dreadful situation in countries where child work is a necessary **source of income** for most families and where going to school is unaffordable.

Even if several conventions[1] ratified by many countries already officially **bar** children from work, as statistics show, it is not enough. More global strategies have to be devised to put an end to the **plight** of so many helpless victims and win back childhood for the world's labouring children.

1 ILO Convention 138 (setting a minimum age for employment 25 years ago). 1989 UN Convention on the Rights of the Child (article 32). 1995 and 1997 ILO's International Programme on the Elimination of Child Labor (IPEC).

Nike Vows No More Child Labor

They just did it. Nike today handed a major victory to labor activists by **pledging** improved labor conditions at its Third World factories and raising the minimum age of employees at its sports-shoe factories to 18. 'Nike has been the poster child for U.S. corporate labor practices in the Third World,' says Time business editor Bill Sapporito.

Time

Ethical shopping

Clothes manufacturers have also become enthusiastic labellers. An American opinion survey in 1995 found that 78% of those polled would avoid shopping in a store that sold garments made with sweatshop labour, and that they would pay a dollar more on a $20 item for a guarantee that the product came from a worker-friendly supplier. In real life consumers might not be quite so meticulous, but companies would rather not run the risk of arousing their ire.

The Economist

Red light

She says an unscrupulous neighbor lured her to Calcutta, and sold her for $30 to a brothel keeper. The child was drugged, **raped** and put to work in the sex trade. 'I used to cry all the time,' she recalls. 'These men, 10 to 15 in a day, would come visit me.' Whenever she managed to scrape up a little cash, a gang of local punks would bully her, rough her up and sexually humiliate her, she says: 'If I protested they would not only take away my money but stub out cigarettes on my face and arms.'

Newsweek

Hunger's Silent Victims

It quickly becomes apparent that the heart of the problem is mind-numbing poverty. 'I had no choice. I had no other way except to send my children away,' says Hol Ny, her eyes wet with tears. The 40-year-old widow, bereft of land or cattle, recently allowed three of her six children to go work for other families, some of them total strangers; the $15 she received per child must feed her and her three youngest for the next year. Hol Ny's neighbor, a 41-year-old divorcée named Pich Mom, sold her two sons for two years each. 'I was sick and couldn't earn any money,' she says. 'It's hard for me to live without my children, but I think I did what was best for them.'

Newsweek

Saving children from sex

Wherever children live in poverty, they are at risk of commercial sexual exploitation. Their exploiters often include visitors from rich countries. Guided by word of mouth or by information on the Internet, sex tourists may behave abroad as they would never dare to behave in their own countries.

The Economist

The Power of Publicity

Human-rights **NGOs** have become highly skilled at media relations, and were among the first of the campaigning groups to embrace the Internet. Every government now must take their views into account. In October Robin Cook, Britain's foreign secretary, appointed officials from Amnesty and Save the Children to work at the Foreign Office.

The Economist

THÈME

1. L'esclavage ne disparaîtra que lorsque les peines encourues seront plus lourdes que les avantages qu'il procure.
2. L'organisation de bienfaisance britannique a mis en garde les consommateurs contre un boycott international. Quand les patrons des ateliers du Bangladesh seront contraints de renvoyer les enfants qu'ils emploient, beaucoup d'entre eux seront obligés de se prostituer ou mourront de faim.
3. Maintenant que la télévision nous livre chaque jour des histoires déchirantes et des images choquantes des jeunes victimes, la prise de conscience et les mouvements de protestation concernant les violations des droits de l'homme sont plus susceptibles de s'intensifier que de s'affaiblir.
4. Suite à des critiques à l'égard de ses fournisseurs en Asie, Reebok s'est engagé à ne pas avoir recours au travail des enfants ou à la servitude pour dette, et, depuis 10 ans, l'entreprise offre chaque année une récompense aux militants qui défendent les droits de l'homme.
5. Les entreprises autrefois rejetaient les critiques en disant qu'ils n'avaient pas d'emprise sur les conditions de travail dans le Tiers Monde et que, de toute façon, la politique n'était pas leur affaire. Cela ne suffit plus.
6. Les détaillants occidentaux ne gagnent souvent que très peu d'argent à faire faire les vêtements par des enfants, même si ceux-ci perçoivent des salaires beaucoup plus bas que ceux des adultes. Ce sont les intermédiaires locaux qui empochent les bénéfices.
7. Il s'avéra que cet homme politique bien connu avait été arrêté au moins deux fois auparavant pour maltraitance d'enfants.

VERSION

1. Many rich countries are making an effort to scare - or shame - their citizens into behaving decently abroad.
2. The emergence of AIDS has played a large role in entrapping more and more children in sexual slavery. Brothel customers aware of the risks of infection want young girls from the countryside who are presumed less likely to have HIV.
3. Over the past 20 years hundreds of human-rights NGOs have been formed to document and publicise abuses, chivy governments into introducing legal change and arouse public opinion.
4. Multinationals are also contracting out an increasing proportion of their production to low-wage countries to help cut costs.
5. Adding grist to the mill of activists, shareholders now want firms they invest in to put human rights into their corporate ethic.
6. Pakistan, for example, has lost $10m as a result of big European carpet importers scrapping orders for hand-knotted rugs.
7. Only when poor countries care more about protecting their children than their tourist revenues will this nasty global trade start to die.
8. A rescue operation secured the release of 17 bonded child carpet weavers. Most of the children could not say how long they had been held captive, but some said they had been working there for three years.

1. Slavery will not disappear until the penalties for it outweigh its rewards.
2. The British charity warned consumers against an international boycott. When sweatshop owners in Bangladesh are pressured to fire child labourers, many of them will have to become prostitutes or will starve.
3. Now that television daily delivers heartrending stories and graphic images of the young victims, public awareness of and protest against human-rights abuses are more likely to grow than fade.
4. After criticism about its suppliers in Asia, Reebok pledged not to use child or bonded labour, and for the past 10 years the company has made annual awards to human-rights campaigners.
5. Firms used to brush off criticism saying that they had no control over third-world working conditions, and that politics was none of their business anyway. This is no longer good enough.
6. Western retailers usually gain very little by having their clothes made by children, even though they are paid far lower wages than adults. It is the local middlemen who pocket the profit.
7. This well-known politician turned out to have been arrested at least twice for child abuse.

1. Beaucoup de pays riches font des efforts pour obliger leur ressortissants à bien se comporter à l'étranger, soit en leur faisant peur, soit en leur faisant honte.
2. L'apparition du Sida a largement contribué à ce qu'un nombre croissant d'enfants se retrouvent victimes de l'esclavage sexuel. Les clients des maisons de tolérance, conscients des risques d'infection veulent des fillettes originaires de la campagne, supposées moins susceptibles d'être séropositives.
3. Ces 20 dernières années ont vu la création de centaines d'ONG qui ont vocation de réunir et de porter à la connaissance du public des documents concernant les violations des droits de l'homme, de harceler les gouvernements pour qu'ils mettent en place des réformes juridiques, et d'alerter l'opinion publique.
4. Les multinationales sous-traitent une partie de plus en plus importante de leur production dans des pays où la main d'œuvre est bon marché pour essayer de réduire les coûts.
5. Les actionnaires exigent maintenant que les entreprises dans lesquelles ils investissent inscrivent les droits de l'homme dans leur politique d'entreprise, ce qui apporte de l'eau au moulin des militants.
6. Le Pakistan, par exemple, a perdu 10 millions de dollars parce que les gros importateurs de tapis en Europe ont annulé les commandes de tapis fait main.
7. Ce n'est que lorsque les pays pauvres se soucieront plus de protéger leurs enfants et moins des revenus du tourisme que cet épouvantable commerce international commencera à péricliter.
8. Une opération de sauvetage a permis de libérer 17 enfants esclaves employés à tisser des tapis. La plupart de ces enfants ne pouvaient pas dire depuis combien de temps ils étaient prisonniers mais certains ont déclaré qu'ils travaillaient là depuis trois ans.

VOCABULARY

abduct (to)	*enlever*
abuse (physical or sexual)	*violences (physiques ou sexuelles), maltraitance*
AIDS	*Sida*
appalling conditions	*conditions effroyables*
ban (to)	*interdire*
bar someone from doing something (to)	*empêcher quelqu'un de faire quelque chose*
beg (to)	*mendier*
bonded labour	*servitude pour dette*
a brand	*marque*
a bribe	*pot-de-vin*
a brothel	*maison de tolérance, maison close*
a child labourer	*enfant qui travaille*
code of conduct	*code de bonne conduite*
contract out (to)	*sous-traiter*
a corporate image	*image de l'entreprise*
dire poverty	*extrême pauvreté*
enforce the law (to)	*faire respecter la loi*
ethical shopping	*achats éthiques*
free market economy	*économie de marché*
HIV positive	*séropositif*
human rights	*droits de l'homme*
human rights abuse	*violation des droits de l'homme*
ILO (International Labor Organization)	*BIT (Bureau International du Travail)*
the IMF (International Monetary Fund)	*FMI (Fonds Monétaire International)*
income	*revenu*
a label	*étiquette*
lure (to)	*attirer (par la ruse)*
a middleman	*intermédiaire*
a migrant farmworker	*travailleur agricole saisonnier*
an NGO (non-governmental organisation)	*ONG (Organisation Non Gouvernementale)*
pledge (to)	*s'engager à, promettre*
a plight	*situation critique*
rape (to)	*violer*
relocate (to)	*délocaliser*
a scourge	*fléau*
sell into prostitution (to)	*vendre comme prostitué*
the service industry	*secteur tertiaire*
the sex industry	*secteur de la prostitution et de la pornographie*
a sex worker	*prostitué (pour ne pas utiliser 'prostitute', politiquement incorrect)*
slavery	*esclavage*
an STD (Sexually Transmitted Disease)	*MST (Maladie Sexuellement Transmissible)*
a supplier	*fournisseur*
a sweatshop	*atelier clandestin*
turn a blind eye to something (to)	*fermer les yeux sur quelque chose*
welfare	*bien-être, aide sociale*
the World Bank	*la Banque Mondiale*

Who's responsible?

- parents? trapped in the vicious circle of poverty.
- consumers, particularly in the sex industry (local customers and sex tourists from Western countries).
- **law enforcement** officials (the police) often accused of accepting **bribes** (corruption).
- the legal system: Paradoxically, legislation **banning** child labour means that children cannot be protected against dreadful working conditions as their work is illegal anyway.
- sweatshop owners and **middlemen** who make a hefty profit.
- companies which **contract out** and **relocate** in developing countries to lower production costs.
- more generally globalisation and the **free market** logic demanding competitiveness and ever decreasing costs.
- The World Bank and the IMF by insisting on a balanced budget and slashing social spending.

What can be done?

- Human-rights organisations campaign:
  - for a more adequate legislation as the existing one has proved ineffective;
  - for a budget **to enforce** the existing laws (well-paid and numerous inspectors);
  - for alternatives to child labour being offered to developing countries, financed by developed countries: new and better schools to make education available to all -girls and boys alike, financial compensation given to families in which children are back to school, better job opportunities and higher wages for adults.
- Organisations committed to putting an end to child labour are UNICEF, ILO (International Labor Organization), the CLC (Child Labor Organization) and the NCL (National Consumers League) in the U.S.
- The Global March Against Child Labor: Launched in early 1998, it started from Asia, Rio de Janeiro and The Cape of Good Hope, the various branches converged in Geneva in June 1998 for the ILO Conference.
- The International Day of the Child (to raise public awareness).

Ethical shopping

FOR

- **Ethical shopping**, buying only from companies which make sure their third word **suppliers** do not abuse human-rights, is a way to force companies to care for children's **welfare**.
- When companies are reported to be guilty of abuses they lose so many customers that many pledge to abide by voluntary **codes of conduct** in order to improve their **corporate image**: Nike, Reebok, Benetton, Levi's, Ikea... Many brands sold in America now carry a label declaring: 'No child or slave labor used on this product.'
- Rugmark (the first human-rights **label**): Created in India in 1994 following a consumer boycott, it certifies that the carpet manufacturer does not use child labour.
- In France 'De l'éthique sur l'étiquette': Many **brands** have entered negotiations to participate in the project (Auchan, Carrefour, Décathlon).

AGAINST

- Some alleged that if children are no longer employed in the formal economy (factories and plantations), they will be worse off, forced **to beg** on the street or lured into illegal sectors such as drug dealing and prostitution.

CLONING
LE CLONAGE

FACTSHEET

Cloning is a commonplace and natural phenomenon which involves the production of duplicate copies of **genetic material**, **cells**, or entire multicellular living organisms. For example, bacteria or single-celled animals are the **offspring** clones of their ancestors. Identical **twins** in humans are clones as well, in that they are produced from the same fertilized egg and are therefore genetically identical.

Artificial **cloning** for agricultural purposes has long been a focus of attention in science and many varieties of fruit and vegetables owe their uniformity of taste, appearance and other characteristics to **cloning**.

As for artificial human **cloning**, until 1996, human clones were primarily a subject of fantasy and science fiction.

However, in 1996, the successful **cloning** of Dolly, the first **mammal** ever cloned from an adult cell **raised** serious concern among the scientific community as well as the general public.

With Dolly, it became clear that the **cloning** of people was a definite possiblity. In theory, **cloning** a human being is even a relatively simple matter.

How to clone?

Cloning is based on **nuclear transfer**, the same technique scientists have used for some years to copy animals from embryonic **cells**.

A human clone could be formed by combining the cytoplasm of an unfertilised egg with the **genetic material** from an adult **cell**. The result would set off a chain of chemical reactions that would eventually result in an **embryo**. That **embryo** would then be implanted in a woman, who would, if everything went normally, have a child nine months later.

So far no human clones have been created but everybody agrees that it is only a question of time. Scientists all over the world are busy working on creating human clones. In fact, in December 1998, a Korean scientist, Dr Bo-Yen Lee even claimed he had succeeded in doing so. For legal reasons the **experiment** was put to an end but Dr Bo-Yen Lee is determined to **resume** the **experiment** as soon as human **cloning** is legal in his country.

Although **cloning raises** a number of ethical issues, it seems that nothing can prevent it from taking place. Now that genetically modified and copied **mammals** are a reality, biomedical **researchers** are starting to develop imaginative ways to use this technology.

How to clone a human being

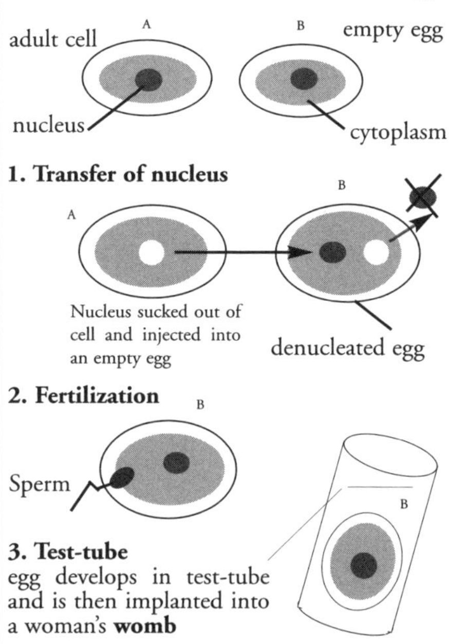

Cloning for human babies must never happen, says poll

Human **cloning** for reproductive purposes should never be allowed, according to public opinion. Those taking part in the **survey**, were almost unanimous in their **abhorrence** of the technique of reproduction without men.
Even most infertile women, those, who had lost children, and lesbians, were opposed. However some felt that it was inevitable.

The Daily Telegraph

US Scientist reveals plan to clone himself

An American scientist who intends to clone himself in an attempt to prove that **genetic engineering** can be a good thing, has said that in future he hopes to make as many as 500 human clones a year. Dr Richard Seed, a Harvard biologist, has said that any attempts to stop the progress of science are **pointless**, and that people should embrace the benefits of cloning rather than worrying about its negative aspects. Parliament can't stop it. Congress can't stop it.

The Sunday Telegraph

Cloning for medicine by Ian Wilmut

The power to make animals with precisely engineered genetic constitution could also be employed more directly in cell based therapies for important illnesses.
Some of the most ambitious projects envision the production of universal human **donor** cells… scientists are learning how to differentiate **stem cells** in culture, so it may be possible to manufacture cells to repair or replace tissue damaged by illness.

Scientific American

Much of the froth of moral indignation generated by the idea of human clones appears to be derived from some very bad movies. *The Boys from Brazil* depicted crazed scientists such as Dr Seed cloning hundreds of Hitlers in the Brazilian jungle. The word clone is associated with the creation of full-blown replicas of evil Nazis.

The Sunday Telegraph

Dolly, You're history

By making dozens of copies of a mouse, scientists take **cloning** one step closer to the **assembly line**. In the year and a half since Scottish embryologist Ian Wilmut presented Dolly, the cloned sheep, to an astonished world, ethicists and **policymakers** have been struggling with the unsettling implications of his research. Could scientists use Wilmut's method to clone not just sheep but also billionaires, basketball players and bodies grown for **spare parts?** Should medical entrepreneurs be allowed to pursue **cloning** wherever it leads? Or should the government **step in** now and outlaw it before it starts?

Time

Human embryos 'cloned within a year'

British scientists could be preparing to clone human embryos within a year to develop new treatments for disease… The government is expected to approve the research following advice from a committee of experts… The report recommended that **cloning** be allowed to develop 'therapeutic treatments for diseased or damaged tissues or organs'. This approach could lead to the production of **'spare part'** tissue grown from **embryo cells**.'

The Daily Telegraph

EXTRA!!! CLASSI-FILES EXTRA!!!

THÈME

1. Ce qui distingue Dolly des animaux clonés avant elle, c'est qu'elle fut clonée à partir de cellules adultes, c'est-à-dire de cellules différenciées.
2. Aux États-Unis, un projet de loi interdisant le clonage humain à partir de la technique utilisée pour la création de Dolly a été rejeté.
3. Des sociétés américaines comme Geron explorent la possibilité de créer des embryons humains à partir de cellules d'adulte, par la méthode de transfert de noyau qui a préludé à la naissance de la fameuse brebis Dolly et de quelques souris et vaches, puis utiliser ces "embryons-clones" pour obtenir des cellules de tous types.
4. L'intérêt de la manipulation, baptisée "clonage thérapeutique", serait immense au plan médical.
5. En effet, les cellules générées à partir de l'embryon-clone d'un malade ne devraient pas provoquer de rejet, une fois greffées : elles ont le même patrimoine génétique que le patient et sont donc parfaitement compatible au plan immunitaire.
6. Autrement dit, avoir son clone au congélateur serait, dans les prochaines années, la meilleure assurance contre la maladie.
7. L'objectif est de fabriquer des embryons humains pour créer des pièces de rechange. La culture de cellules embryonnaires humaines aurait donc une visée thérapeutique.

EXTRA!!! CLASSI-FILES EXTRA!!!

VERSION

1. It is conceivable that a human with a failing liver could have a new one grown from, say, a cell taken out of his bone-marrow.
2. Cloning will allow us to grow replica embryos of an individual in a laboratory and we can then harvest the tissues or organs to replace defective nerves or kidneys.
3. Creating a carbon copy of a living adult will, however, always be impossible.The difference in age between parent and child alone would prevent it. What is more, because genetics only partly determines who we are, a clone could never be exactly the same person as its parent.
4. The offspring of a brilliant musician or a scientific genius could turn out to be a great criminal.
5. But human cloning will happen anyway, perhaps much sooner than anyone thought.
6. The first person to suggest cloning might be possible and worthy of pursuit was a German scientist who, in 1938, suggested removing the nucleus, which contains the genes, from an egg and replacing it with the nucleus from another cell.
7. It might be possible in future to make cells develop into bone marrow, skin or nerves. In the more distant future it may even be possible to make organs such as liver and kidneys.

1. What distinguishes Dolly from previously cloned animals is that she was cloned from adult cells, that is to say, from differentiated cells.
2. In the United States, a bill banning human cloning using the technique employed to create Dolly has been rejected.
3. American companies such as Geron, are studying the possibility of growing human embryos from adult cells using the method of nuclear transfer which led to the birth of the famous ewe, Dolly, and to that of a few mice and cows, in order to then use these cloned embryos to obtain all sorts of cells.
4. The medical benefits of such a manipulation, called 'therapeutic cloning', would be enormous.
5. Indeed, the cells grown from a patient's cloned embryo should not trigger rejection once grafted as they have the same genetic make-up as the patient and are therefore fully compatible with the body's immune system.
6. In other words, in years to come, having one's own clone in the freezer would be the best health insurance policy.
7. The aim is to produce human embryos in order to manufacture spare parts. The purpose of the culture of human embryonic cells would therefore be therapeutic.

1. Il est concevable qu'une personne ayant un foie déficient puisse s'en faire créer un nouveau à partir, disons, d'une cellule prélevée de sa moelle osseuse.
2. Le clonage nous permettra de créer en laboratoire des répliques d'embryon d'un individu et nous pourrons ensuite récolter les tissus et organes afin de remplacer les nerfs ou reins déficients.
3. Créer le double parfait d'un adulte vivant sera, cependant, à jamais impossible. A elle seule la différence d'âge entre le parent et l'enfant l'empêcherait. Qui plus est, parce que la génétique ne détermine que partiellement qui nous sommes, un clone ne pourra jamais être tout à fait la même personne que son parent.
4. La progéniture d'un brillant musicien ou d'un génie scientifique pourrait s'avérer être un grand criminel.
5. Le clonage humain aura lieu quoiqu'il arrive, peut-être bien plus tôt qu'on ne s'accorde à le penser.
6. La première personne à suggérer que le clonage était réalisable et digne d'intérêt fut un scientifique allemand qui, en 1938, émit l'idée de retirer le nucleus – ce qui contient les gènes – d'un œuf et de le remplacer par le nucleus d'une autre cellule.
7. il est envisageable qu'à l'avenir on fasse en sorte que des cellules se développent en moelle osseuse, peau ou nerf. Dans un avenir plus lointain encore, il est possible qu'on soit même en mesure de fabriquer des organes tels que le foie ou les reins.

VOCABULARY

abhorrence	*répulsion, aversion*
assembly line	*chaîne de montage*
assess	*évaluer*
ban (to)	*interdire*
bone-marrow	*moelle osseuse*
breakthrough	*grande découverte, avancée*
breed (to)	*se reproduire, une espèce*
carbon copy	*copie parfaite*
cells differentiated/undifferentiated	*cellules différenciées/indifférenciées*
cloning	*clonage*
defect/defective	*défaut, anomalie, déficience/déficient*
donor	*donneur*
DNA	*ADN*
embryo	*embryon*
endanger (to)	*mettre en danger*
experiment	*expérience*
effective	*efficace*
gene	*gène*
genetic blueprint, genetic make-up, genetic material	*patrimoine génétique*
genetic engineering	*génie génétique*
genome	*génome*
graft	*greffe*
harvest (to)	*récolter*
kidneys	*reins*
law-abiding	*respectueux des lois*
liver	*foie*
mammals	*mammifère*
nuclear transfer	*transfert de nucléus*
nucleus	*nucléus,noyau*
offspring	*progéniture*
outlaw (to)	*rendre illégal*
pointless	*vain, inutile*
policymakers	*décideurs*
raise concern (to)	*soulever des inquiétudes*
rejection	*rejet*
researcher	*chercheur*
resume (to)	*reprendre, recommencer*
scientist/scientific	*scientifique*
spare parts	*pièces de rechange*
species	*espèce*
Stem cell	*cellule souche*
step in (to)	*intervenir*
survey	*enquête, étude*
test-tube	*éprouvette*
transplant	*transplantation*
trigger (to)	*provoquer, déclencher*
twins	*jumeaux, jumelles*
unsettling	*inquiétant, qui perturbe*
womb	*utérus*

The arguments for and against cloning

FOR

■ Thanks to **cloning** many diseases could be avoided and many lives could be saved.
- Animals could be genetically engineered to produce human organs or valuable human proteins. For example, pigs whose organs have been altered to remove proteins that **trigger rejection** after **transplant** operations, could be stamped out on an **assembly line.**
- **Cloning** will allow us to grow replica embryos of an individual in a laboratory and we can then harvest the tissues or organs to replace **defective** nerves or **kidneys**.
- Most of us regard all such meddling with nature as a technological step too far. So why don't scientists just respect public opinion? Suppose we put the lid on the whole thing. Every time that a child died of leukemia for want of a matched **bone-marrow** donor, the death would be on our consciences.

■ **Cloning** will offer the possibility of children to couples who would otherwise be unable to have them.
- It would be impossible to produce true duplicates of people. Most **genes** provide potential, but experience and environment determine if and to what degree this potential is realised. If Michael Jordan were cloned, it is very uncertain that his clone would achieve much as a basketball player if he did not have the extraordinary support that Michael Jordan got from his parents.

■ Farmers could have herds of ideal farm animals efficiently producing milk, meat, and eggs of just the type desired.
- Fast race horses or blue-ribbon pets might be duplicated at will.

AGAINST

■ **Cloning** is unethical, morally repugnant and contrary to the respect for the person.

■ As unexpected developments occur, we may fear that cloning might **endanger** our survival or that of some species of animals.
- An issue of concern is the effect that a large population of clones - human or otherwise - would have on evolution. One advantage to having a wide variety of genes within a species is that when something like a new disease develops, some individuals may have a **gene** or genes useful in surviving the new challenge. Such a **gene** or genes, though previously not particularly useful and not likely to have been selected for duplication in **cloning**, might save the **species** from extinction.

■ Cloning human beings might have unwanted consequences.
- Cloning could enable mad scientists to create thousands of Hitlers.
- Clones of **law-abiding,** virtuous people could develop into criminals or develop vices the originals never had or were able to control.

Achevé d'imprimer en août 1999
dans les ateliers de Normandie Roto Impression s.a.
61250 Lonrai
N° d'impression : 991888
Dépôt légal : août 1999